Privatization in the Developing World

Privatization in the Developing World

L. GRAY COWAN

PRAEGER

New York
Westport, Connecticut
London

Library of Congress Cataloging-in-Publication Data

Cowan, L. Gray (Laing Gray)
   Privatization in the developing world / L. Gray Cowan.
   p.   cm.
   Includes bibliographical references and index.
   ISBN 0–275–93631–7 (alk. paper)
   1. Privatization—Developing countries. I. Title.
HD4420.8.C69 1990b
338.9′009172′4—dc20   90–7573

A hardcover edition of *Privatization in the Developing World* is available from
Greenwood Press (Contributions in Economics and Economic History, Number 112;
ISBN: 0–313–27330–8)

Library of Congress Catalog Card Number: 90–7573
ISBN: 0–275–93631–7

First published in 1990

Praeger Publishers, One Madison Avenue, New York, NY 10010
An imprint of Greenwood Publishing Group, Inc.

Printed in the United States of America

The paper used in this book complies with the
Permanent Paper Standard issued by the National
Information Standards Organization (Z39.48–1984).

10   9   8   7   6   5   4   3   2   1

Contents

Preface

The mounting financial problems faced by countries of the developing world over the past decade have forced many governments to consider reducing the role of the state in economic activity by divestment to the private sector of enterprises operated by the government. The growing acceptance of privatization derives in part from the gradual ideological change that has taken place in many countries since independence from colonial rule and in part from external pressures for reform that have been applied by bilateral and international donor agencies. The examples of successful privatization as a means of achieving higher productivity and lower costs in the industrialized world have not been lost on the developing countries. But perhaps the strongest driving force has been that more governments are facing the reality that, unless subsidy costs to money-losing industries are drastically reduced, the financial burden they create will become unsustainable.

With broader acceptance of privatization has come increased knowledge of the process it entails and greater sophistication in dealing with the problems that it may present for the governments. The initial concentration on divestment of industries has given way to greater attention to privatizating in other sectors of the economy, most particularly in agriculture and in the services formerly made available to the public by the government alone.

This combination of a greater understanding of the advantages to be gained from privatization and its wider application has led to a "second phase" in the privatizing process. No longer is it necessary to present the concept of privatizing to government officials in the third world nor to argue its philosophical merits; such knowledge can increasingly be taken for granted. Rather, the concerns of governments focus more specifically on acquiring a detailed knowledge of the "how-to" of privatizing. These concerns include, among others, preparation of the firms for eventual disposition; more realistic valuation by the governments, in the light of current market conditions, of the industries they seek to sell to private buyers; alternative methods of carrying out the sale; and more sophisticated ways in which the privatization transaction can be financed. Until recently externally supplied technical assistance has provided much of the nuts-and-bolts information needed by officials in the developing world to initiate a privatization strategy. But, increasingly, governments wish to develop their own plans with the help of local civil servants without relying on external advice.

Although some principles regarding the privatization process can be universally applied, each country must be treated as an individual case by taking into account local circumstances. Opposition to privatizing both by political parties and interest groups must be dealt with, and legal and financial institutions must be developed to meet the new problems privatization creates. Although advice may be needed on how to meet opposition arguments, the solution to the political, institutional, and legal problems faced by the government must be sought locally by those most familiar with the country.

The purpose of this volume is to supply a basic text on privatization techniques and methods for the use of government officers in the developing world whose task it is to devise the government's strategy for a privatization program and to implement the decision to divest. Each of the topics treated requires further expansion in its application to the particular conditions of private sector activity and capital market development of the country as well as to the macroeconomic policy environment in which privatization is to take place. It is hoped that the case histories of actual developing world privatizations will provide examples of ways in which special problems have already been met and that the solutions may be adaptable to particular local conditions faced by countries embarking on privatization for the first time. In part, the discussion of some of these problems has appeared in somewhat different form in papers and memoranda prepared by the author for the Bureau for Program and Policy Coordination of the United States Agency for International Development (U.S.A.I.D).

My collecting of material on privatization has been greatly assisted by many conversations with government officials of developing countries and officers of U.S.A.I.D. missions all over the world and with those who have undertaken privatizations in the United Kingdom. Staff members of U.S.A.I.D. in Washington, particularly Edward Lijewski of the Bureau, have reviewed the text, and I am grateful for their comments. Andrea Love and Edward LaFarge of the Scientex/Center for Privatization have been equally generous with their help in research and critical reading. Michael Field and Baljit Vohra, the center's research assistants, corrected many textual flaws.

My greatest debt, however, is owed to Neal S. Zank, senior policy adviser in the Resource Policy Division of the bureau. I have benefited greatly, both in style and content, from his critical reading of various versions of the text and from his broad knowledge, not only of privatization, but of private sector development in the developing world. Without his help, the volume would have been much the poorer.

Errors of fact and of interpretation remain, as always, my own responsibility.

Privatization
in the
Developing
World

1

Introduction

THE BACKGROUND TO PRIVATIZATION

Over the past three decades state-owned enterprises (SOEs) have played a grow-ing and, in some cases, pervasive role in the economies of developing countries. The number of public enterprises mushroomed as did their share in production and service activities. In Mexico and Brazil, for example, SOEs quadrupled in slightly more than twenty years. The World Bank has estimated that there are well over three thousand SOEs in sub-Saharan Africa alone.

While there is no universally agreed upon definition of a public enterprise, the term is generally used to mean any government-owned or controlled unit that produces and sells industrial, commercial, or financial goods to the public. This definition does not, however, distinguish between wholly state-owned en-terprises and those in which the state shares majority or minority equity with private sector owners. Public enterprises include not only those producing specific products but organizations such as agricultural or commodity marketing boards involved in both regulating commerce and in operating commercial marketing and input activities themselves.

SOEs took on a wide variety of forms over the years, depending on the state of development of the country and the government's commitment to state own-ership and control of the means of production. They may be categorized as:

- Enterprises wholly owned and operated by the state. In some cases these tended to be capital and/or technology intensive operations that were regarded as essential to eco-nomic progress or to national security, such as mining or petroleum production.
- Enterprises partially owned by the state and partially by private sector investors. The term "parastatals" is sometimes applied to this category of enterprise, but there is no generally accepted usage. The form and degree of control exercised over these enter-prises varied widely. In some cases it was related to the size of the government's

holding; in others to the ideological stance of the ruling party or the perceived need to control assets for national security reasons.

- Enterprises owned by government but operated by outside managers.

- Public services owned and provided by governments, local or national. These included railways, telecommunications networks, national airlines, and national health and educational services. At the municipal level they included transportation, refuse disposal, markets, and a variety of other local services.

THE RISE OF THE STATE-OWNED SECTOR

The growth of the state-owned sector since 1960 is attributable in part to the colonial experience during which a foreign administration directed the bulk of economic activity. In the post-independence years, state domination of the economy was accepted since this was the system to which the new governments were accustomed. After independence there often remained a deep-seated suspicion of the motives of the private sector stemming from foreign control of industrial and agricultural development. Moreover, in many countries popular resentment existed of resident ethnic minorities (as, for example, in Kenya and in Southeast Asia) who had exercised control over the distributive sector before independence. There were also both ideological and practical elements to the growth of state control. Socialism was a reaction to the capitalism of the colonial powers; ownership by the state was generally seen, moreover, as the only way to preserve economic independence in the face of a perceived threat of neocolonialism.

In some cases governments backed into state ownership more or less by default as private sector firms seen as important to development failed, either through mismanagement or corruption, and the state was forced to assume control (as, for example, in the case of the Philippines). Labor unions were often more content to deal with the state rather than private sector owners, and the private sector was happy to have the state take the risk, especially in capital intensive industries.

The basis for state ownership often rested on purely pragmatic factors. In many countries, the government concluded that the private sector had neither the capital nor the technical and managerial skills to establish new industries, especially where these industries were designed as part of an import substitution program. In some cases, the failure of the private sector to respond to what the government felt were good investment opportunities was not perceived for what it really was—lack of interest because of too little profit potential and too high an investment risk. Political exigencies required the government to find jobs in the modern economy for the new urban populations and, at another level, to provide management and board sinecures in return for past political favors or military service. SOEs were not infrequently justified publicly on national security grounds; it was too risky to entrust vital food supplies or the needs of the armed forces to private sector producers.

In theory, SOEs were expected to produce profits that would then be ploughed back into new development projects by the government; this expectation was only rarely fulfilled, indeed, in some less developed countries (LDCs) privatization has even been considered as a means of creating new resources designed to develop more SOEs. State enterprises, particularly export or import monopolies, were created to stabilize agricultural prices, to provide subsidized consumer prices, or even to collect taxes. SOEs frequently satisfied the perceived need for rapid indigenization of the modern sector of the economy and allowed the state to maintain the stance that it was the protector of the interests of the popular majority against rapacious private exploiters, foreign and domestic. Politically, the proliferation of SOEs enhanced the consolidation of political power in a single party together with control over the developing economies of the post-independence regimes. Moreover, they provided a fertile field for the growth of special interest groups.

THE FAILURE OF STATE-OWNED ENTERPRISES

Over the more than three decades of national independence in the developing world, enterprises owned by the state have produced a staggering burden of subsidy costs for their governments. SOE borrowing on the international market added substantially to the overall national debt. The growing numbers of state enterprises and their expansion into new fields of endeavor brought LDC governments to the realization that they had created a monster that could devour them.

The World Bank (1983) has highlighted the budgetary costs of SOEs. A sample of developing countries showed that net budgetary payment to nonfinancial SOEs averaged more than 3 percent of gross domestic product (GDP)—in some cases, much more; in Sri Lanka, 11 percent; in Zimbabwe, more than 10 percent. A 5 percent increase in SOE revenues and a 5 percent decrease in their costs would have been enough to finance all of Tanzania's expenditures on health and education; similar changes would have financed two-thirds of Mali's outlays on education and twice those on health.

So long as the market for their primary products remained reasonably buoyant and development was supported by external donors, LDC governments could continue to enjoy the luxury of high subsidization. But growing demands on national revenues for increased public services and new infrastructure combined in the mid-seventies with the sharp rise in petroleum prices to add urgency to the search for relief. LDC governments were reaching the limits of domestic taxation of agricultural and mineral production while mounting debt service payments and foreign exchange shortages added to the crisis.

The growing indebtedness of SOEs derived from several sources:

• Many governments were prone to use them for other purposes than those for which they were originally designed. Conflicting objectives—social and financial—brought conflicting signals from the government so that management was unable to determine what policies were required to meet these objectives.

- Inexperienced management was unable to operate the businesses profitably. The blame cannot, of course, be placed entirely on management since government pricing and labor policies not infrequently made it impossible for even an efficient manager to overcome the social overhead costs the firm was required to bear. In many cases the manager was asked to produce results from a firm that had been located for political or regional development reasons with little thought to its proximity to markets or accessibility of raw materials. The result was that the national treasury had to make up for the growing negative cash flow if the SOEs were to continue in business.

- Many governments failed to develop effective means for monitoring the numbers and performance of SOEs. Partly as a result of uncoordinated donor assistance, projects were often initiated through several ministries. There was often little firm information on the exact number of enterprises the government owned. In the course of an inquiry, the Kenyan government, for example, found that it had an interest in some four hundred enterprises; the Ministry of Finance was unaware of many of them. The governments were also unaware of the extent of the debts that they had guaranteed in loans to SOEs. They were slow to realize the dangers posed by SOE indebtedness, which in many cases accounted for 20 percent to 40 percent of total domestic credit. Between 1976 and 1983, SOEs were responsible for $80 billion of LDC debt.

In the absence of standardized accounting methods, measurement of SOE profitability was often difficult. An interesting attempt was made by the Experts Advisory Cell in Pakistan to measure the profitability of forty-three selected SOEs as compared to a similar number of industries in the private sector producing the same products. Data was drawn from profit and loss statements of the firms over a number of years, with adjustments made for the peculiar handicaps under which the SOEs operated as compared to firms subject only to market forces. Pakistan was fortunate in having this data available; few other countries are in this position.

Some governments went to opposite extremes in control over their SOEs. In some cases monitoring was so loose that there was no detailed knowledge of the fiscal state of the enterprise. In others, monitoring by government ministries was so close that management lost almost all autonomy in day-to-day decision making. Having to refer operating decisions to the ministry's representative created a serious bottleneck to increased productivity.

Official estimates of expenditure on subsidies were often unrealistic or erroneous. Subsidies continued to be paid for political reasons when they could no longer be justified on economic grounds, and little serious thought was given to their ultimate impact on the financial structure of the country's SOEs. Subsidy costs extended far beyond the explicit costs appearing in line items of the government's budget. Implicit subsidies were concealed in many obscure government accounts. Gillis (1989) has pointed out that the cost of these implicit subsidies may take the form of receipts forgone by an SOE or the government, such as reduced SOE profits, unpaid taxes, and "equity injections" by the government to cover operating losses of SOEs. Not included in overt subsidy programs, for example, were government guarantees of SOE incurred foreign borrowing that was viewed by the lender as sovereign debt. SOEs also had preferential access to domestic credit, often on highly concessional terms.

According to Gillis, SOE sector deficits in developing countries were estimated at 3 percent of GDP in the late 1970s but were probably as high as 5.5 percent when implied subsidies were taken into account. By the early 1980s, SOE debts rose as high as 10-12 percent of GDP in some countries. A further form of implicit subsidy derives from SOE import privileges and the "tax-like" subsidies, to use Gillis's term, that come from the failure of SOEs to pay other SOEs for services rendered. In Jamaica, the government-owned electric company was finally pushed to the point where it threatened to cut off service to government ministries because of their failure to pay electricity bills. More than one LDC national airline has been forced to bankruptcy because government officials refused to pay for tickets.

Factors beyond the control of LDC governments also contributed to the failure of the SOEs. After having been encouraged by the willingness of public and private foreign lenders to provide capital to establish state enterprises, many governments found that the loans that had once been so readily available were being drastically reduced by the early 1980s. The foreign exchange reserves that many former colonies had built up prior to independence were exhausted, frequently as the result of investment in ill-advised industrial expansion projects that were part of an import substitution program or construction that served only to reinforce the vanity of the new political leaders. Markets for LDC primary products declined, new competitors were entering fields that had formerly had few producers, and technological advances were making the equipment of many SOEs obsolete. They could no longer produce at competitive prices so their attractiveness in import substitution programs was reduced.

Reducing SOE deficits became, therefore, a national priority; the solution was seen to be divestment or liquidation of money losers. Contracting out of management in an effort to bring the firms to a break-even point in the hope of attracting a future buyer, or at least eliminating the need for subsidy, was one possible alternative. Some governments accepted the idea that, by creating competition for SOEs through encouragement of private sector enterprises in the same field, the need for SOEs could be eliminated.

The alternative to divestment was to raise consumer prices of SOE products and services, if the firms were to continue in business, to a point where the consequent public unrest could call the political survival of the government into question. The long-range goal was to harness more effectively the energies of the private sector to better meet the growing popular demand for high quality consumer goods and services. Privatization was also seen by some governments as a way to bring much needed income to the national Treasury by sale of public assets.

By the late 1970s, ideology was beginning to be less of an obstacle to reducing the role of the public sector. Socialist doctrines had failed to effectively mobilize and sustain community resources and popular energies for development; on the contrary they had impeded development by repressing individual initiative, especially in agriculture. The cautious search for pragmatic solutions to the governments' financial problems through greater reliance on the private entrepreneur found support in unexpected socialist quarters such as China and Hungary. In Africa such staunch socialists as the late Sékou Toure in Guinea and Julius Nyerere in Tanzania finally admitted that mistakes had been made in village collectivization programs.

But divestiture of money losing SOEs did not prove simple. Disposal of firms both deeply indebted and with negative cash flow was all the more difficult when there was serious disagreement between the government and prospective buyers on the value of the firm. The public sector's heaviest losers were often natural monopolies, such as railroads and electric power generation facilities, which were the least likely candidates for divestment.

DEFINING PRIVATIZATION

Privatization may be defined as the transfer of a function, activity, or organization from the public to the private sector. The concept is not new; it can be found in the writing of Adam Smith as early as 1762. The great trading companies of the early period of European empire building, such as the British South Africa Company and the Dutch East Indies Company, were in private hands until they were taken over by governments as part of the rise of global foreign policy interests in the imperialism of the nineteenth century.

The current renewal of interest in privatization is a phenomenon mainly of the late seventies and early eighties. It became a matter of national policy in the United Kingdom with the coming to power of the Thatcher government, which undertook the largest privatizations ever to take place—British Telecommunications and British Gas. Privatization efforts have spread throughout Western Europe, particularly France, but not as extensively as in the United Kingdom.

Privatization is a relatively new term—its first appearance in a dictionary came in 1983. With increased usage, its meaning has broadened to include the economic setting in which privatization occurs, since the environment in which the private sector is required to operate is an essential element in successful privatization.

The process of privatization may assume a number of forms. In complete divestiture, publicly owned assets may be completely transferred by sale to private individuals or firms after which the government bears no further responsibility for the operation of the assets. This is the clearest and most desirable form of privatization, but is often the most difficult to accomplish.

Alternatively, in partial divestiture, the state retains partial ownership of the divested assets by selling a portion to individual buyers either directly or by means of a public stock flotation. The proportion divested may leave the government with either a majority or minority share, but the practical effect is to put the current operation of the firm or service in the hands of private managers; the government remains a shareholder with representation on the board. Partial divestment, or mixed ownership, creates special problems that will be discussed later.

The assets may also be removed from direct control of the government by management contracting, leasing, or franchising. Management contracting puts operations in the hands of an outside management group while leaving ownership in government hands; its major purpose (as is the case with leasing or franchising) is to restore an ailing firm to profitability. This may be part of a long-range plan leading to complete privatization when, and if, the firm becomes an attractive candidate for sale.

A variation on the leasing arrangement, known as the contract plan, has been employed in France and French-speaking Africa. Here the government draws up an agreement (usually lasting three to five years) with the management of an SOE that specifies in detail performance standards that the SOE is expected to meet and for which the managers will be held responsible. Failure to meet the standards will raise the question of management change if it can be determined that the fault lay with management rather than with extraneous causes over which management had no control.

Wholly owned subsidiaries of a larger SOE, or of services within vertically integrated firms (such as importation and retail distribution of fertilizer), may be achieved by a process of spinning off. Examples include construction of transmission stations within a national telecommunications system or establishment of airport services and duty free shops under a national airport authority.

2

Developing a Strategy for Privatization

INITIAL CONSIDERATIONS—WHY PRIVATIZE?

An official expression of interest in privatizing on the part of the government is usually the first step in initiating a planned program. This interest can sometimes be sparked through discreet urgings by international or bilateral donor agencies or the local private sector. Pointing out the advantages of privatization as a solution to some of the pressing financial problems of the country's Treasury and explaining the privatizing process may inspire the decision to proceed. Citation of examples of successful privatization in situations similar to the circumstances of the country concerned may be helpful.

In the final analysis, a combination of carrot and stick may be required to prompt the government to action. Clear communication by donor agencies and private international commercial banks that failure to reduce the public sector burden on the national budget will result in decreased assistance is usually a decisive factor. Privatization may be made a requirement in negotiations for an IBRD (International Bank for Reconstruction and Development) structural adjustment loan. It may also be stressed in policy dialogue on fundamental economic policy change or in negotiations on rescheduling outstanding external private loans to foreign banks. In any case, the decision to seek technical assistance on reducing the public sector has to be made at the highest levels of government.

Motivations for Privatization

A careful analysis of what has led the government to contemplate privatization at this particular time is usually necessary. It is important that the motives of the government in seeking assistance for a privatization strategy be carefully evaluated in advance of any offer to help because they can influence the techniques of divestment and sale that may be utilized. The following factors are among those that play a role:

- A growing awareness of the deficits created by mounting subsidy costs that may be reaching a crisis point. If the interest in privatization is simply a function of the desire to reduce the costs of public sector enterprises, then it is unlikely that privatization will progress rapidly enough to permit sizable and immediate reduction of either debt or subsidies. The government should be aware that it cannot expect immediate or miraculous budgetary results from divestment.

- The government may view privatization primarily as a source of additional revenue for the Treasury from the sale of state-owned assets. Sales will occasionally bring immediate and substantial returns (as in the case of the privatization of the National Commercial Bank of Jamaica). But these will frequently be less than expected if the government has inflated notions of the value of the assets being divested. In any case, revenues from the sales will be slow to come in and initial privatizations may be of relatively small firms.

- Some governments see profits from sales as a potential way to avoid, or at least reduce, a rise in tax rates. The British government, for example, has been accused by the opposition of masking its real reason for privatizing, i.e, to curry favor with the electorate by keeping taxes low.

- The interest in privatization may reflect a genuine concern on the part of government to reduce the public sector or just a reluctant response to pressures exerted by external agencies. If real political will is lacking, foot-dragging bureaucratic delays can be anticipated, and requests to finance all or part of the preparatory planning as well as sales will be made to donor agencies.

- General dissatisfaction with the performance of SOEs may be a force for change. They may have failed to meet popular expectations for product quality or quantity. They may be too ambitious in their product lines or unable to deliver on time. They may be unable to compete with already flourishing private sector competition (as in the case of petrochemical subsidiaries of Petrobras in Brazil or the Heavy Mechanical Complex in Pakistan, where a private company produced better quality products) or with imports (even where duty is paid). Technological advances may be making the product or service provided by an SOE obsolete, and changing world markets or differing consumer tastes may be making a product more difficult to market. The government may therefore feel that privatization can be justified as a result of consumer demand.

A full understanding of what is involved in privatization will take time on the part of government officials, but the effort will be well repaid if it enables the process to go smoothly later.

THE POLITICAL FACTOR IN PRIVATIZATION

The decision to embark on a privatization program is based as much on political factors as on financial and economic considerations. It is of the highest importance that the government analyze closely the political impediments to privatizing and the ways by which these impediments may be eliminated, or at least minimized, in planning a privatization strategy. The case studies of Jamaica and Costa Rica demonstrate the relationship between political problems and the approaches used for their resolution.

Any decision to privatize involves a degree of risk for a government. The problem lies in reducing the risk to a politically acceptable level while still leaving the government in a position to achieve a successful privatization program. If outside agencies require too high a level of risk in return for their aid in privatizing, the government may refuse to act or, more likely, prolong the preparatory process to the point where privatization becomes impossible. Simply changing ownership does not provide all the answers; unless the change is accompanied by deregulation and policy reform, the benefits of private sector investment and management will be severely reduced. In the final analysis, the spread of privatization will depend on the ability of the political leadership of a country to demonstrate concrete benefits from privatization to the public at large. Only in this way will a constituency be created that will ultimately guarantee an expanded role for the private sector.

The degree of political risk deriving from the decision to privatize is directly related to the type of regime under which the country is governed. The more groups or individuals whose interests may be threatened by privatizing, the greater the risk. Although it may be possible to alleviate the fears of many of these interested parties, there will always remain those who refuse to accept the concept of privatization out of ideological conviction. It is doubtful that rational persuasion will change their position or eliminate their opposition; the government may have to take the calculated risk that its appeal for privatization will never be accepted. If little or no economic opportunity exists outside the political arena, the government will approach any potential threat of defeat with extreme caution. If privatizing means serious reduction in optional funds or perquisites available to those in power, it may be totally rejected even though the assets being privatized are losing money.

A one-party system, of the type commonly found in Africa, faces increased risk in divesting state-owned industries even if it does not have a political opposition to cope with. As Goren Hyden (1987:26) has pointed out, political order in one-party states often depends on the ability of the head of the government to have discretionary use of public revenues for political purposes.

Maintaining a regime while privatizing may require negotiation with powerful party or ethnic interests, compromise in bureaucratic positions, and answers to ministerial objections. Depending on the charisma and strength of the party leader, these may not prove to be critical barriers if, as in the case of Malawi, for example, the government can count on widespread public support. Successful privatization in a one-party system may be a matter of overcoming popular suspicion of the private sector by keeping the process transparent.

The highest level of risk comes in a multiparty democratic system in which the governing party may put its political existence at stake if its privatization program is not a demonstrable success. The greater the degree to which the government depends on popular choice, the more attention that has to be paid to detailed planning and public education before privatization can become a reality.

The regime that risks least in deciding to privatize is a military government. In this case, the decision can be taken by fiat from the top with little or no forced consultation with any group. As long as the interests of the military are not put in jeopardy (by privatization, for example, of firms seen to involve national security) there is likely to be little outcry except from military officers enjoying their SOE board sinecures; arrangements may have to be made ultimately to take care of their concerns. Labor unions' views, on the other hand, are not usually a critical factor in a military regime.

A monarchy, headed by an active ruler with power, risks little in declaring for a privatization program. In Morocco, for example, progress in privatization will depend on the public support given to it by the king. Without this, the bureaucracy will inevitably drag its feet, and the politicians will hesitate to act for fear of incurring royal displeasure. Where the monarch is more of a constitutional figurehead, as in the case of Thailand, the decision to privatize may rest largely with the political leadership.

Sources of Political Risk

There are many groups in the public and private sectors of developing countries that have a vested interest in either the adoption or prevention of a privatization program. These groups may contribute to the political risk faced by an LDC government.

In countries where an institutionalized opposition party exists, a privatization program may become a convenient and effective weapon with which to attack the party in power. Opposition to privatizing from within the ruling party itself may come from factions seeking to embarrass the leadership for reasons having little to do with the privatization issue.

To the degree to which the government is responsive to public opinion, a threat may arise from a groundswell of public resistance to privatization created by the opposition. Political opponents may seek to exploit public ignorance of the meaning of privatization to their advantage before the government is ready to make public its case for privatization. Even in a populist regime, such as that of Jerry Rawlings in Ghana, privatizing will have to produce some immediately evident results, or popular support will decrease rapidly.

Opposition parties may object to privatization for a variety of reasons. One of their accusations may be that of selling assets owned by the people at less than popularly perceived value (the perception often being based on original amounts invested by the government in an enterprise or the enterprise's book value), thereby creating a loss to the taxpayer. In fact, the market value of SOEs is almost invariably less than the amount of government investment in them.

The opposition party may also reap political capital from the charge that assets are being sold to political cronies or through questioning the credibility of those handling the sale by accusing them of bribery and corruption. In other cases, the opposition may appeal to nationalist sentiment based on the dangers of allowing production facilities to fall into the hands of outsiders, such as foreign nationals or multinational firms. Often tied to this accusation is pressure for indigenization, particularly of management positions.

Political objections to privatizing may arise on ideological grounds, particularly in those countries where there was a strong socialist movement in the post-independence period. Although some of the ideological arguments against privatization may grow out of genuine socialist convictions, ideology can also be a convenient screen behind which may be hidden perceived damage to personal interests. The government may even find that it has an ideological mole in its own ranks, so that word of privatization planning in official meetings may be leaked prematurely to fuel opposition arguments.

In countries where there is a strong legislature, the head of the government may have to deal with the possible defeat of privatization legislation on a vote. If the government's majority is slim, the ability of the opposition to swing a few votes (through an appeal to personal interests) may defeat the privatization strategy. Indeed, if the privatization legislation is considered sufficiently critical, the opposition may use it as a threat to overthrow the regime. This can be a very high risk factor in countries where politics is still a zero-sum game.

Political questions in privatization do not end with sale to the private buyer. It will be of little advantage to the political leadership if the sale results only in substituting a private monopoly for a public one, from which there is no guarantee of greater efficiency, more competition, or cheaper, better quality consumer products. The government may, in fact, lose credibility with the voters, and its opponents may gain, if it appears that the sale was engineered to give special advantage to a chosen private sector group. Based on its own past experience, the Moroccan private sector, for example, has reservations about privatization for this reason.

In any regime, interest groups are an important political factor, no matter how tightly political power is controlled. Even in the military governments, factions within the military itself may become interest groups. In democratic regimes, interest groups both within and outside of the ruling party play a significant role in maintenance of party support.

Privatization presents an opportunity for interest groups to exert a variety of pressures on the government, since privatization may ultimately affect broad strata of society. The greater the degree to which the government is dependent on support of special interest groups, such as organized labor, the greater the threat of group opposition to the maintenance of power.

Opposition from within the bureaucracy, for example, can be a critical impediment to privatization planning, especially if an alliance can be struck between bureaucrats and the opposition party or opposition factions within the majority party. Bureaucratic interest group objection may stem from genuine ideological objection to the disposal of SOEs; more likely, however, privatization may be seen as a threat to both position and power. Ministry officials who exercise direct control over SOE budgets and operations may resent the diminution of their status and power. If ministry representatives occupy board seats on SOEs, they may lose not only perquisites and position but directors' fees and sitting expenses paid to board members. It is easy to see, for example, why in Indonesia the young administrators who represent the minister of finance on the boards of important SOEs—each one sits on several—may not be proponents of privatization since loss of board seats would be a loss of an important status symbol. Included in bureaucratic opposition are the current managers of SOEs who may lose their positions under new ownership.

Bureaucratic opposition can be particularly risky and difficult to overcome, since it is often clandestine, as opposed to the opposition of the more vocal interest groups in the public sector. The bureaucracy can derail a carefully planned strategy, discourage potential buyers, and create public suspicion of the government's intentions through a combination of losing files, scheduling endless meetings, and procrastinating in issuing directives.

The military in many countries constitutes a special interest group that opposes privatization, ostensibly on national security grounds. The military may argue that products of SOEs are required for military supply and that security would be threatened if the military were forced to depend on privately owned sources. This argument against privatization rests on somewhat spurious grounds, since most governments retain the power to requisition production facilities in case of a national emergency. The real grounds for opposition may be that retired or active officers sit as members of SOE boards (as in the case of many Indonesian SOEs); privatization would result in personal financial loss as it would indeed to former politicians in the same position. In countries where politics is one of the most lucrative sources of income, the possibility of such appointments may be critical to party support by influential local figures.

Labor is a special interest group with substantial political strength in many countries. Labor may oppose privatization in countries such as Indonesia, for example, where the SOEs have been used as a substitute for a government operated social security system; not only loss of jobs but also of pensions may be at stake in privatization. If the government receives labor support and union leaders choose to use their muscle to oppose privatization, the degree of political risk grows. Minimizing the risk from labor opposition will be dealt with in a subsequent section.

There is also the risk of alienating parts of the private sector; privatization is not always regarded as an advantage by the more prominent entrepreneurs. In many developing countries, firms with close relations to the government may have benefited from the same privileges that were extended to SOEs— particularly in freedom from import restrictions, greater access to foreign markets, and reduced competition. Some large private sector firms may find their position undermined by the new competition introduced from privatized firms.

Economic Factors in Political Risk

Privatization may also present economic risks that translate into political risks for the government. Several governments have hesitated to embark on privatizing because of fear of losing control of the pace and direction of development, especially in the industrial sector; thereby, exposing themselves to the charge of sacrificing the popular welfare to the private profit motive. Even if the charge is without foundation, the perception carries considerable political weight.

The government may be blamed for consumer price rises that occur when a formerly state-owned enterprise is privatized and is then subject to market forces in the pricing of its products. Violent upswings in prices of consumer staples may trigger political upheavals that threaten the ability of the regime to govern or remain in office.

Finally, privatization is not without direct financial cost to the treasury, even if donor technical assistance is available. If fiscal demands regularly outrun resources, as is the case in many African countries, the initial cost of privatizing may be more than the government is prepared to bear, especially if high priced investment banking advice will be needed. It may be necessary to demonstrate that the cost of such advice is still less than the subsidy cost of maintaining an SOE. Opposition charges of squandering scarce resources on foreign advisers for the doubtful purpose of privatizing may be difficult for the government to counter if it cannot prove that advice on privatizing is cheaper than continued subsidization. It is also important that the government realizes that long-term tax revenues from increased production and profits from privatized SOEs can compensate in considerable part for the costs of initial advice.

Many LDC governments lack experience in the use of regulatory powers that may serve to blunt criticism of privatization. The political leadership should be aware that, in privatizing an industry considered essential to the public welfare (such as a public utility), the government retains the power to regulate pricing of the product in the public interest should this appear necessary. An understanding of the use of this power can serve to reduce the risk of selling so-called "strategic" industries.

After the sale of an enterprise the government must assure itself that the terms of sale are observed, that payments are made in accordance with the agreed schedule, and that labor retention covenants are kept. If the private buyer fails to live up to his commitments, the government may be placed in the difficult position of having to take back the privatized industry, adding fuel to the opposition argument that privatization does not work.

For a privatization program to be successful, the government must demonstrate that its decision to privatize is a firm, long-term policy. If potential buyers suspect that there is even a remote possibility of renationalization, they will be unwilling to risk capital to buy divested industries. Should the impression be created that the government's decision to privatize could be overthrown by an opposition party at a forthcoming election, the offerings will find few takers. On the other hand, if enough privatizations are completed with clear benefits to stockholders and the public, more supporters of further privatization will be created to counter opposition arguments (as the case of privatization of public housing in the United Kingdom amply illustrates). Privatizing carries its political rewards as well as risks; the problem is to impress the public with the benefits of privatization in order to create lasting support for a long-term program.

Reducing Political Risk from Party Opposition

The top leadership of a government must be determined to privatize if organized party opposition is to be effectively met. As illustrated by the situation in Honduras, consistent public commitment by the head of the government helps to ensure passage of privatization legislation. The move toward privatizing the generation of electric power in Pakistan was in part attributable to the prime minister's public statements of commitment to the idea.

There is often a political element in the choice of the method to be used for privatization. The government has several options at its disposal to reduce risk in privatizing. If, for example, one of the government's motives in divestment is to redistribute wealth in the community, an obvious option is a stock market offering directed particularly to the small investor. By limiting the number of shares any one individual may acquire, a constituency for privatization can be created as well as a ready market for the next offering. As the privatization of the National Commercial Bank of Jamaica illustrates, the government may gain political advantage by pricing the share offering at a level that will produce immediate gains to purchasers.

Should the enterprise be too large for a single buyer, a consortium of local buyers may be created for a joint venture. Alternatively, a joint venture may be formed with foreign equity participation, in which local buyers play a dominant and public role. If there is a strong current of public opinion opposed to foreign acquisition of enterprises, emphasis can be placed on assisting local buyers to find the necessary capital to buy divested industries. In some countries, certain families or traditional authorities play crucial (albeit unobtrusive) roles, even though they may not be part of the institutionalized political structure. They may have to be identified and brought quietly into the information network when planning is being undertaken, since they may themselves constitute sources of capital for privatization and have contacts with foreign capital sources that they may be prepared to use for privatization ventures.

It may appear politically desirable that the government retain a minority holding in a divested firm in order to avoid the accusation of selling out the public interest. For example, in the case of the Togolese steel mill, it was clear that the current market value of the firm was much less than the government's investment in the firm. A market value sale would have constituted a serious embarrassment to the political leadership. To avoid this situation, a foreign management contractor was permitted to operate the firm under a complex contract agreement that paid the operator a share of the profits.

If the government elects to retain a minority share, it should be encouraged to keep its holding as small as possible and to commit itself to ultimate full privatization as political circumstances change. In many developing countries any firm dealing with the basic food supply of the country is often regarded as being of strategic national concern; as a result the government may never be able to afford to relinquish full control to any private operator.

Exclusion of some ethnic groups from competition in privatization is a highly sensitive political question that can only be approached delicately by outside advisors. Unless some way around it is found, however, the privatization process may be seriously impeded. In the case of Kenya, for example, one possible solution suggested was to restrict the sale of shares offered on the market to Africans but to allow Indians to assume management of the firm under contract once the sale had been completed. The government thus could not be accused of selling to the Indian minority, but the management and entrepreneurial skills of the Indian could be utilized to improve the performance of the divested firm. Such a formula might be applicable to other countries in which the ethnic problem plays a role.

A campaign of public information and education on the meaning and advantages of privatization in support of the government's policy can be used effectively to mobilize public support prior to any sale. Such a campaign can utilize published material and radio and television broadcasts designed to create a greater public understanding of privatization. The general public should be informed of the government's privatization plans as soon as they are reasonably well formulated. If the public perceives the privatization as shrouded in official secrecy, it is more likely to react against it no matter what its advantages. Opposition interests can exploit the popular feeling that deals are being made to the advantage of politicians and high government officials. The government should explain its motives and make clear why certain industries and not others are being singled out for privatization. The steps that are being taken to ensure that members of the public are not being harmed should particularly be emphasized.

It is of major importance that the government's announcement of privatization plans be carefully timed to minimize political risk. A detailed plan should be well thought through by the top political leaders, identifying major program objectives and incorporating a flexible timetable for achieving specific goals, before any publicity appears. In the United Kingdom, for example, the privatization of the domestic water supply had to be indefinitely delayed because of premature announcement without consultation with consumers who feared a steep rise in water rates would result. The plan should not be so completely cast in concrete that the government cannot respond to public reaction by making changes that will allay popular fears.

Even though there may be an element of public relations involved, it is essential that the public be allowed to express opinions as the privatization strategy evolves, preferably before or at points where it is possible to demonstrate that changes are being made in response to public objections. Privatization will be more readily accepted if the government is able to create the feeling that it is paying attention to legitimate objections being raised and is sincere in dealing with them.

It is important to demonstrate publicly at an early stage that privatization can produce concrete and visible beneficial results. It may be politically advantageous to go forward with a particular privatization that gives prospect of immediate success in terms of quick or easy sale. Such a sale can be useful to convince the opposition of the benefits of privatizing, even though it may not produce the largest return. In some cases, temporary leasing of facilities (such as hotels in the Philippines or Jamaica) may be an easy way to facilitate the move toward privatization without raising the political problems attendant on complete public sale. Technical assistance can provide advice to governments on which enterprises should be given priority in privatizing.

Internal political considerations may determine the precise timing of a privatization. If the government is operating in a period of crisis or has made policy decisions that create public unrest (such as a sharp increase in the price of food), the privatization may have to be delayed until officials can concentrate on the sale process. Too frequent sale offerings that decrease private sector liquidity or overtax the institutional capacity of financial or legal institutions may produce a dearth of buyers. Failure to bring about a successful sale only serves to confirm opposition arguments that privatization is undesirable.

Interest Group Opposition and Political Risk

Interest groups may be as much a threat to privatization as are political parties. If interest groups are allied with opposition parties, the degree of risk may be even greater. But interest group opposition can be dealt with and reduced depending on the particular concerns of the group.

Overcoming bureaucratic opposition is a matter of firm and persistent pressure by the political leadership. It will be necessary to enforce on ministry staffs rigid deadlines for detailed planning and to brush aside spurious reasons for delay. Ultimately, threat of demotion or firing may be required if it appears that some high officials are determined to dig in their heels but the risk grows proportionately if this becomes necessary.

Alternatively, privatization planning may have to be removed from the usual ministry channels and put in the hands of a specially appointed group of committed and loyal civil servants (a privatization secretariat) that reports directly to the head of state and is empowered to override any objection or delaying tactic. There may be argument within the bureaucracy itself over which ministry or agency should be charged with the privatization mission (as between Finance and Planning, for example). In such a case, the head of the government, with cabinet support, may have to make a final decision and be prepared to enforce it.

If the military has sufficient political influence, it may be necessary to retain some active or retired officers (and politicians) on the boards of privatized firms, simply as a cost of successful privatization. If this is the case, provisions for this may have to be included in the terms of sale to the private buyer. The special situation of the labor movement as an interest group also has to be kept in mind in this context.

Opposition from current SOE managers may be reduced by assurances that competent managers will retain their positions under privatization; indeed, the good managers will prefer to remain in their posts if it appears that they will be given greater autonomy in operating the firm. Some board sinecures may have to be retained to soften opposition. Bureaucrats who no can longer sit on SOE boards as government representatives can be hired as part of the new management team of the privatized firm if they are competent to handle the jobs. They may be especially useful as liaisons between the firm and the government.

The government needs detailed knowledge regarding the size and constituency of the political opposition and of its ability to mobilize its followers. If the arguments that it may use can be ascertained in advance, it is possible for the government to have counterarguments prepared, tailored to the positions of special interest groups. For example, the standard argument of the threat to national security made by the military can be met by early consultation with the most senior staff officers to ensure continuing sources of military supplies from privatized firms as part of the sale agreement.

Reducing Risk with External Assistance

Donor advice and technical assistance in the political field on privatization is an especially delicate matter. There is a fine line between offering advice that may be necessary to ensure that political objections do not upset the privatization strategy and being accused of interference in the internal affairs of the country; advice on overcoming political impediments should be tendered only on request. Acceptance of the advice depends on establishment of a firm and lasting relationship of trust with the political leadership and demonstration that donor support of privatization is long term. Suggestions as to suitable specialists to hire with technical assistance funds can be made, but the final choice of consultants rests with the government. Donor influence is limited by the fact that privatization is essentially a sensitive domestic issue in which too much evidence of outside interest may do more harm than good.

To be most effective in assisting the government to make the decision to embark on privatization, the donor needs detailed knowledge of the political system and the environment in which the government operates. Some of the elements to be considered are:

- Where does political power really lie and to what extent is it exercised independently of group interests or popular consent? Who is normally consulted before an important political decision is made?
- What is the interest (professed or real) of the opposition in objecting to privatization? Is opposition to privatization merely a smoke screen for an ulterior motive? What is the real strength of the opposition's ideological position, and how much public support is there for it?
- What real degree of risk is the government taking in privatizing as opposed to the risk it perceives—and what elements of this risk are susceptible to change as a result of outside pressure or advice? To what degree is political risk balanced by the need to reduce the subsidy burden or modernize public sector industries?
- Does the government want to restrict, for internal political reasons, the range of buyers, excluding some groups as unacceptable buyers?

Apart from establishing a consistent and comfortable relationship with the major government officials concerned, the donor will have to judge the rate at which the government is prepared to proceed with privatization. The process is invariably slow; perfectly reasonable technical advice may be ignored or tabled for political reasons that are neither obvious nor easily understood by the outsider.

There is a danger that in the enthusiasm to press forward with privatization, the donor may give the appearance of getting out ahead of the government or of public opinion. The impression that pressure is being applied to encourage quicker action may be resented publicly by the government, even though officials may privately be in agreement that some pressure is necessary. It may also be important to be sure that all elements, political and bureaucratic, understand the technical assistance being offered, especially if the privatization action depends on enabling bills being enacted by the legislature.

No government wants to be seen as giving way to outside pressure in its decision making. Successful privatization may often depend on convincing the public that the program is a purely governmental initiative. Consultants should make it clear that they are in the service of the government alone. Only then will the government be assured that the advice being given is in the country's interests. Some governments make explicitly clear that privatization decisions are an exclusively internal matter by excluding donors from any role in them.

Political decision makers are apt to consider privatization plans more seriously if they contain a variety of options rather than recommending a single course of action. Being given a choice allows the political leadership to make up its own mind on the one technique with which it is most at ease politically and avoids the perception that it is being forced to accept advice dictated from the outside.

At the same time the donor has to avoid giving the impression that it is delaying if the government appears to wish to proceed more rapidly. Before extending an offer of technical assistance, the donor should be sure that the necessary specialized consultants are available so that the gap between acceptance of the assistance and its implementation is as short as possible. Reports or other data should be submitted to the appropriate government office in final form and on schedule—even though it may be obvious that action on recommendations may not be forthcoming for some time. It is highly desirable that a single individual on the donor's staff be responsible for the work on privatization over as long a period as possible so that government officials have a known reference point when the need arises.

Estimating the rate at which the government wishes to advance the privatizing procedure may be a major factor in planning technical assistance. Low key advice at the right time is usually far more effective than a hard sell approach that preaches the virtues of privatization; the latter may, in fact, have a serious boomerang effect. The government will be more receptive to advice that stresses the difficulties and pitfalls as well as the advantages in privatizing.

The government may be prepared to accept external technical assistance and advice from some donors but not from others or may refuse any advice from international bodies. A foreign private sector firm with which the government is acquainted may be encouraged to provide the technical assistance needed for privatization. This may serve to avoid some internal political hurdles because the government can point to the source of the advice as being disinterested, particularly if the foreign firm is excluded from becoming a possible bidder for a firm scheduled for divestiture.

In the case of Sierra Leone, for example, the government opposed turning to the World Bank for assistance in privatization because it resented the conditionality accompanying that assistance and because it questioned whether the bank would be able to furnish the kind of business advice that was needed.

Instead, the government turned to a multinational firm with heavy investment in the country and with which it felt comfortable, believing that the private sector firm was likely to give more hardheaded and expert advice on the divestment of SOEs than could any donor. The advantage to the multinational firm is that it serves to reinforce the firm's position with the government if questions of concern to the firm's own business later arise. In Malawi, an investment coordinator with private sector experience was employed with donor help and given substantial responsibility to negotiate sales of firms being privatized.

Before technical assistance is offered by donors, the government should commit itself to permitting private sector competition with privatized firms. Any appearance that a privatized firm will continue to receive special treatment after the sale will seriously undermine any claim by the government that it is seeking to strengthen the private sector and the free market system. Privatization actions in the Philippines are a case in point; here the government had to be careful that sales of post-Marcos SOEs did not expose it to the accusation that a new cronyism was being allowed to emerge. A stock offering sale, even though resulting in immediate gain to purchasers, but with subsequent deterioration of service to consumers, could undermine favorable public reaction to the whole privatization plan.

Donor assistance, if properly handled, can play a crucial role in developing the privatization strategy. The exact nature of this role depends, of course, on the particular circumstances of each country; few generalizations can be made that apply across the board. Over the years donors have provided the resources that have led to industrialization as well as to advances in agriculture and as a result have accumulated a stock of knowledge of the developing countries and their resources, people, and capabilities.

If the government has built up confidence in their past work, donor officers can often be in a favored position to suggest changes in the public-private mix, and when the government is prepared to make these changes, to prepare the way for privatization. They can be a source of basic information on the entire process at the initial stages, explaining the fiscal advantages of privatization while at the same time pointing out the pitfalls that may result from inadequate planning, and can offer advice on the choice of units to be divested and on the process through which divestment can take place.

At the second phase, preparation for sale, donors can furnish the technical assistance necessary for evaluation of a company, provide the legal preparation for change of ownership, and locate suitable buyers. They can play a dual role as disinterested participants in assisting both the buyer and the seller in negotiating mutually agreeable terms of sale.

Not all donor advice is likely to be palatable to the government. The technical advisers provided may suggest liquidation of an SOE as unsaleable, meaning almost total loss of the investment already made.

Debt encumbrance may be an insurmountable obstacle to finding a buyer for many companies that are candidates for privatization. If the government is not capable of discharging SOE debt and labor obligations before divestment, it may seek donor financing to implement privatization. In this case, the limits of donor contribution should be made clear to the government from the outset, otherwise there is a risk that the whole program will be rejected at a later point. Once committed to assisting a privatization program, a donor cannot afford to reduce its contribution without seriously damaging its credibility; planning of donor resources over the expected period of the privatization plan is necessary.

It is important that bilateral donors establish and maintain close coordination with field representatives of international donor agencies if duplication of effort and overlapping of assistance is to be avoided. Assistance with privatization is a part of the lending programs of the World Bank and the International Finance Corporation. In the case of Morocco, for example, a substantial World Bank loan has been negotiated for rehabilitation of public sector industries, part of which will be eventually used to further privatization.

Privatization is such an important and long-term decision on the part of a government that if donor agencies are to become involved, they must be seen to be in full and continuous support of it as a long-range goal. Officers designated as liaisons with officials dealing with privatization should be able to give their full attention to the question, not just on a part-time *ad hoc* assignment basis. When personnel changes are made, donors should try to name successors who have substantive skills in privatization in order to maintain the government's confidence in donor support.

The donor may desire to proceed with privatization more rapidly than local political circumstances permit. Estimating the most desirable pace requires familiarity with the local decision-making process and the personalities involved. Privatizing is inevitably slow and complicated; too much pressure on a privatization secretariat to move quickly only produces irritation and too little gives the impression that the donor may be losing interest. The sentiment of the private sector will have to be gauged as well. Too much pressure to use available local capital for privatization may produce a choking-off effect, to the detriment of new ventures that may be contemplated by private entrepreneurs.

The donor's role in privatization is not confined to assistance with the planning and mechanics of the privatizing process, since successful divestment depends heavily on the broader economic context within which it will be carried out. There is little point in pushing privatization if the environment in which the private sector is forced to operate is clearly not sympathetic to individual initiative. For most LDCs, especially those that have been subjected to a regime of state socialism over more than two decades, fundamental changes in both macro- and microeconomic policies will be needed before the private sector can be persuaded to take on new risks. A period of confidence building may be required before local entrepreneurs are convinced that the government will allow markets to operate with relative freedom and that the danger of renationalization of privatized firms with a change of political regime is minimized.

These fears are not confined to the LDCs; privatization in the United Kingdom was beset from the first by doubts as to the intentions of the opposition Labour party should it regain power. Labour made no secret of its desire to reverse the major privatizations undertaken by the Conservative government. As divestment proceeded, however, it became clear that a constituency in favor of privatizing was rapidly being built among the new shareholders of privatized firms. Apart from the fact that the cost of regaining government control over former SOEs was likely to be beyond the resources of any newly elected government, large segments of the public were converted to support of the privatization program regardless of the party in power.

Privatization is only one part of reducing the role of the state in the economy. The government must be willing to accept profound and far-reaching policy changes as part of the process of integrating the private sector more fully into the economy. Convincing the leadership to initiate these changes may require extended policy dialogue by donor agencies, in most cases preceding or as part of discussion on the decision to privatize. For many leaders who have been accustomed to state management of the economy, change will not come easily. Easing of government controls means reducing bureaucratic power and, in the view of those who still retain deeply engrained suspicion of the private entrepreneur, there is the perceived danger of allowing the development process to get into the hands of those who seek to turn it to private profit.

Necessary long-term structural changes at the macroeconomic level may include:

- Encouraging the development of expanded domestic capital and stock markets through greater sophistication in finance on the part of the local private sector. Establishment of a stock market (as in the case of Thailand, Barbados, Jamaica, and Kenya) may be an appropriate mechanism even if the number of companies registered is very small. Privatization may contribute to the growth of a nascent capital market by presenting new opportunities for local investors with available capital. With capital and stock market growth, enterprises may be created to compete with money-losing SOEs, ultimately eliminating them as competitors. Donor agencies can provide the technical assistance where needed to create the stock market. In countries where lack of equities in domestic hands does not allow a stock market, other financial instruments may be used to finance privatization.

- Liberalization of foreign exchange restrictions so that the private sector can be assured of equitable access to foreign exchange for modernization of equipment and purchase of raw materials while preferred access by SOEs to foreign exchange is eliminated.

- Encouragement of expanded credit facilities available to the private sector through intermediate financial institutions. These should be able to supply the medium- and long-term credit necessary for the creation of new enterprises or for the purchase of privatized SOEs, in contrast to the short-term credit preferred by commercial lending institutions. Lending by the Multilateral Development Banks (MDBs) in Asia, Latin America, and Africa directly to the private sector without government guarantee has been cautiously undertaken in Asia but has not yet received enthusiastic support from the other regional banks.

Policy reform has become a major concern of both international and bilateral donors in recent years. Major reform of macroeconomic policies is a political question that has aroused strong passions and substantial controversy in many LDCs; thus far, it has achieved varying degrees of success. Reform programs have often been designed from a purist view of economic rationality, but their execution has important political implications. Without serious long-term government commitment to the changes involved and government capacity to implement the changes, the sustainability of a reform program is questionable.

Nevertheless, growth of the private sector through industrial expansion and privatization depends on reform of the financial structure and of policies favoring the SOEs. Without the higher productivity and greater employment opportunities that growth will create, the private sector has little opportunity to achieve a more positive image in the eyes of the public. Donor help will be essential to achieving major policy changes, but the sensitivity of the issues and the political risk involved requires that the donor, the governments, and the private sector tread warily in undertaking them.

The Institutional Factor in Privatization

As experience with privatization in the LDCs has broadened, it has become increasingly apparent that critical barriers to successful privatization exist in the lack of suitable institutions and institutional capabilities to permit the privatizing process to go forward. Even with the best political will in the world, the transfer of public organizations to private hands is difficult, given the necessity of deciding which companies to privatize, the prices to be sought, and the buyers to choose. Beyond these hurdles, there frequently remain impediments that require changes in constitutional, legislative, and regulatory codes to make privatization more feasible. Barriers exist also in institutional capabilities in developing countries' legal, accounting, and financial systems.

Technical assistance by donor agencies can be of major help in resolving the institutional problems surrounding privatization. The government may need advice on the framing of privatization legislation and the revision of codes to avoid restricting private sector operation, as well as on the making of policy changes designed to provide a more level playing field for the private entrepreneur. Donor help may be needed in creating specific new institutions or agencies, such as privatization secretariats or committees, to advise on and implement the privatization process.

Although countries with similar colonial backgrounds may have the same basic legal frameworks (such as the former French colonies whose systems are based on the Code Napoleon), present-day structures may vary as a result of laws passed since independence. However, changes made in countries where privatization has been initiated may provide adaptable examples for resolution of similar legal problems elsewhere.

Impediments to the Transfer from Public to Private Ownership

Hemming and Mansoor (1988:32) have argued cogently that "privatization is . . . likely to be dominated in economic terms by other policies, in particular liberalization and regulation, and more effective variants of the incentive systems and control mechanisms, both statutory and administrative, concurrently in place." There will undoubtedly be substantial institutional changes as part of programs to encourage the private sector, but it is too early to estimate the effect of these changes. World Bank structural adjustment loans are a strong factor in institutional restructuring. Deregulation and removal of government controls over private sector operation to encourage the growth of competition will make privatization easier. At the same time, new regulatory structures will inevitably be needed to control, for example, environmental impact or industrial safety as the private sector grows. All of these changes are aimed at a reduction in the role of the state from one of controlling economic development to one of monitoring it. They become part of privatization in the larger sense; without these fundamental policy, institutional, and regulatory changes, privatization in the narrower sense of simply disposing of enterprises run by the state will be slow to develop.

Changes in the statutes and codes required to embark on a privatization program in many developing countries are complex and often without precedent. Accomplishing these changes may be cumbersome and time consuming, delaying the privatization process to the point where potential buyers will lose interest. But if at least the most important of these changes are not made before the privatization program is started, the private sector will understandably be reluctant to become engaged in it for fear that legal ownership of the privatized firm may later be challenged or become a matter of judicial determination.

Constitutional Obstacles

Fundamental to initiation of privatization is the determination of whether or not the government has the basic legal power to dispose of publicly owned property without specific legislative or judicial consent. Freedom to dispose of public property may depend on fundamental documents, such as a national constitution. In Portugal, for example, sale of nationalized industries is constitutionally forbidden. The Mexican constitution requires that industries regarded as strategic be state-owned so that sale to the private sector is impossible. Such basic constitutional provisions can only be overcome by changes in the document itself (usually a very difficult process that any government would be hesitant to undertake) or by judicial interpretation, if this is itself constitutionally permitted.

The government's ability to dispose of state-owned industries may also depend upon the origin of the specific industry. If, for example, an industry was nationalized by a previous regime, it may enjoy a statutory position that differs from those industries established by the present government. This was the case of jute mills in Bangladesh that were formerly owned by West Pakistanis.

In Thailand SOEs are divided into two general groups, depending on whether or not they are considered to have a "juridical personality." This, in turn, depends on the arm of government that created them. SOEs that came into existence by royal edict or law, revolutionary council order, and civil or commercial statute have a juridical personality, while those established by cabinet decision do not. These differing legal modes specify the reasons for setting up the enterprise and the powers and duties of boards and managers. The mode has, in turn, implications for privatizing the enterprise. It is very complicated to sell a firm established by royal act; on the other hand, one established by cabinet decision may be divested by a stroke of the pen. Most Thai SOEs of major importance derive their existence from royal or statutory action.

In those countries with a strong executive president system, it may be possible to sidestep some of the legal thickets surrounding the disposal of SOEs by a direct presidential decision that enables ministries to sell firms under their direction. In Malawi, for example, once the life president had agreed to the proposed privatization strategy, any existing legal obstacles were easily overcome. In other countries, such as Tunisia and Honduras, where the legislature plays a substantive role, a privatization law has been passed overriding existing statutory impediments. Such a law may specify individual enterprises, or categories of enterprises, to be privatized or empower the government to make specific decisions under certain general guidelines. It is important, however, that the law be very carefully drafted so that legislative intent is clearly delineated to prevent later objection to actions taken under it or accusation from those who oppose privatization that it was misinterpreted.

Statutory/Legal Impediments

A broad range of statutes affect privatization. To be successful, a privatization program may require changes in laws or regulations that are only indirectly concerned with the enterprises being privatized, such as those governing foreign exchange regulation, the structure of corporate debt, restrictions on private sector operation or ownership, and banks and other financial institutions. Continuing barriers to privatization in many LDCs are statutory codes that act as deterrents to potential investors in SOEs scheduled for privatization. These include, among others, investment, labor, and commercial codes.

Many LDCs, particularly those that are former colonies, have had such codes since before independence, but they are for the most part outmoded and contain provisions no longer applicable to the current stage of the country's development. They have been amended so frequently that they are little more than a hodgepodge of often contradictory regulations, subject to bureaucratic interpretation and hit-or-miss application. The codes have, however, proved useful to often inexperienced and poorly-educated civil servants, who are able to avoid the necessity of making a decision or taking action by hiding behind a maze of regulations. The result is that a foreign investor becomes frustrated and loses interest in the country.

An important area of law for privatization deals with the legal form of an SOE and a private company. Most SOEs cannot be privatized without at least some modification of their legal form to conform to existing statutes governing privately owned firms, as well as modification of operating and management procedures.

In order to fit the newly privatized firm into the provisions of company law, it may be necessary to take legal steps to dissolve the SOE and recreate it under new articles of incorporation. Occasionally, amendment of the existing articles may suffice, but this may be as complicated as reincorporation. Particularly in many Central American countries, company law proves to be a serious barrier to quick privatization in that the consent of all private shareholders in a mixed company must be obtained prior to sale of the government share, and the legal extinction of the firm's juridical personality may be the subject of a prolonged court proceeding.

If mixed ownership has already brought the firm under company law, the government may be able to sell its current holdings without legal complications. Joint ventures between government and foreign shareholders may require modification of statutes governing the proportion of foreign holding permitted in national companies. Clarification of the rights of debtors and existing shareholders may require statutory action before the company becomes privately owned.

Transforming a ministry (which may even have been enshrined in a constitutional provision) or government agency into a private firm is normally accomplished in a series of steps. The first of these requires a legislative act to turn the ministry into a state-owned company. This is followed by a transformation of the concern into a public firm that may be sold to a private investment group or by share offer through a stock market listing. All of these steps require special legal expertise and an in-depth knowledge of constitutional and company law. This procedure is most frequently used in the case of privatizing public utilities, such as telecommunications or electric generating facilities that have hitherto been departments or agencies of the government.

An illustrative case is that of the Malaysian Telephone Company. The PTT Agency, Jabatan Telecom Negara, was first turned into a wholly government-owned company, Telecoms Malaysia Berhad, to which the assets, liabilities, and personnel of the agency were transferred. The second step transformed the new SOE into a public limited firm, with the necessary changes required in accounting and valuation. The final step was listing on the Kualalumpur stock exchange, after a new regulatory framework had been worked out.

Privatization will usually require modification of some aspects of accounting procedures that may be mandated by statute. Government accounting regulations are usually substantially different from those of private business so that reconciling accounts of some SOEs (which are often chaotic in any case) with figures meaningful in a business may create a serious barrier to privatization. Where multinationals are concerned in joint ventures, accounting procedures must meet recognized international standards. Private accounting firms in Tunisia, Algeria, and Morocco recently met to establish common rules and procedures for the area, a task made somewhat easier since the systems of all three are based on standard French practice.

One of the objectives of governments seeking to embark on privatization programs has been to bring the budgeting operations of major parastatals in line with those of the private sector. Parastatals tend to produce budgets late and without adequate documentation. Capital transfers from ministries are off budget, and business development plans are lacking. An example of the effort to correct these defects can be found in the State Corporations Bill passed in Kenya in 1986.

This bill, which applies only to wholly owned state enterprises, provides regulations designed to control and supervise all SOE expenditures in order to prevent the waste and fraud all too prevalent in the past. SOEs are required to maintain a full internal accounting system, and their books are audited annually by the auditor general of corporations. The legislation also provides for the old British colonial device of surcharge, by which executives, as individuals, are held personally responsible for irregularities in accounts under their control; any missing amounts are made up from the individuals' own pockets. Overall performance of the SOEs is monitored by the State Corporations Advisory Committee, composed of high government officials, which has wide powers to advise the president on all aspects of SOE operation. The Government Investments Division of the Treasury is responsible for advising on SOE investments and performance evaluation.

The intent of the bill is clear and its objectives highly desirable, but it raises two questions: (1) does it go too far in prescribing rules for SOE financial decision making so that it becomes an invasion of management autonomy? and (2) does the government have sufficient skilled accounting staff to carry out the monitoring requirements of the bill? Implementation of the terms of the bill will eventually provide the answers. If financial and operational procedures of the SOEs can be brought under greater control using practices comparable to those used in private business, it will make them more attractive to investors in the event that the government should decide to place them on the market.

Limitations Imposed by the Regulatory Framework

Although legislative acts and regulations deriving from executive sources may in some countries make the privatization process slower and more complicated, the corpus of regulations stemming from bureaucratic implementation of legislative intention or from direct exercise of bureaucratic power may provide an equal, if not greater, barrier to easy privatization in most LDCs. Every government exercises its regulatory power to some degree, but in many LDCs regulatory power, particularly at the ministerial level, has been used to hinder investment and industrial development by needlessly complicating proposed actions or by discriminating against particular individuals or firms.

Regulations may be issued to require or forbid specific actions or require the completion of myriad minor steps before an action permitted by statute can be taken. Prime examples are the issuing of export or import licenses, land tenure regulations, and business permits. Meeting regulatory requirements not only takes effort but offers endless opportunities for bureaucratic delays and bribery. No one source knows all the regulations; new and often contradictory restrictions appear to be invented on the spot. As with statutory provisions, regulations can be a convenient cover for failure to act, which really derives from bureaucratic incompetence.

Eventually, the frustrated potential investors may simply take their money elsewhere. The so-called one-stop investment offices created by several developing countries have rarely been successful because ministry officials are reluctant to give up even minor authority in the interests of saving the investor's time. Elimination of many of these petty regulations would simplify the privatizing process and encourage entrepreneurs to concentrate on the profit possibilities of divested firms rather than on the annoyances created in the process of acquisition.

Where privatization occurs in enterprises susceptible to competition, regulation will play an important role. As Marsden and Belot (1987:31) have pointed out:

Clearly the impact of competition policy—and privatization—on the efficiency of private enterprises with dominant positions in potentially contestable markets will depend upon how well the regulatory regime functions. Regulation will also determine the efficiency of privatized natural monopolies. Thus the effect of the current shift in the emphasis of industrial policy toward private competition depends largely on the effectiveness of regulation.

Inducing increased foreign private investment may, in many countries, require liberalization of existing regulatory structures rather than revisions designed to strengthen them. To cite only a few examples:

- Free convertibility of foreign exchange allows market forces to determine its accessibility as opposed to an allocation structure based on complex regulated procedures.
- Removal of regulated price controls provides price incentives for producers, and elimination of wage rates constrained by regulation will permit greater labor market flexibility.
- Reform and simplification of tax codes and regulations to remove distortions prejudicial to the private sector will increase investor confidence.

If regulatory liberalization for the foreign investor is combined with macroeconomic policy changes that enable the private sector to compete on an equal footing with public enterprises, the chance of a successful privatization program will be greater.

A profitable privately operated industry may produce more revenue for the government through well framed and fairly administered tax regulations than even a profitable SOE will produce. LDC governments need more skill and experience in the use of regulatory instruments for tax revenues. These skills can be taught through donor technical assistance for training regulatory agency personnel and taxation specialists. Regulatory and other barriers to foreign investment can be changed through conditions attached to World Bank structural adjustment loans, as has been done, for example, in the Cote d'Ivoire.

Many governments are becoming increasingly concerned about regulatory code provisions that impede free market operations, and outside technical assistance is being sought to rewrite them in their entirety. In most cases priority is given to the investment code because simplifying it is likely to encourage foreign investment and is less apt to provoke internal political objection than is the rewriting of, say, the labor code.

The major objective of any investment code is to demonstrate a stable and regulated environment. Insofar as possible a code should be clear and unambiguous and should apply equally to all investors at all times. Certain automatic rights of investors are written into many revised codes. Marsden and Belot

(1987:31) note that the Guinean code of 1987 is typical in that it provides freedom for private sector firms to:

—import necessary raw materials and equipment and export production;
—set and implement their own employment policies;
—choose their own customers and suppliers, under freely established prices;
—repatriate earnings from imported capital and repatriate liquidated capital; and
—enjoy free competition with parastatal enterprises that should operate under free market conditions.

The code incorporates guarantees of freedom from expropriation unless it is required "in the public interest," in which case fair compensation will be paid. Equal treatment for local and foreign investors, equal patent and trademark protection, and equal access to the judicial system is also built in. Similar clauses were included in the revised code in Madagascar in 1985. These provisions follow generally accepted international standards.

The Guinean investment code is exceptional in that there are no requirements that local investors be part of a joint venture. Other countries have devised joint venture regulations so complex that many investors would be discouraged from embarking on this type of investment.

Most investment codes provide for some type of investor incentive for approved development projects, including exemption from customs duties and income tax for a specific period. Few, however, contain specific incentives for investors in privatized firms; rather they are designed for new investment, although exceptions may be made for rehabilitation investment.

A number of codes have not yet solved the problem of complex and time-consuming investment applications, which often leave room for uncertainty as to whether the prospective investment will ultimately be qualified. There is no doubt that a carefully constructed investment code that measures up to contemporary international standards serves to reassure investors and, therefore, may act to support a privatization program. But the mere existence of a modern code does not necessarily guarantee investor protection or, indeed, investor confidence. The government must gain a reputation for reliability in application of the code and fairness when the courts are called in to decide disputes.

Labor codes in many parts of the developing world are generally designed to provide the fullest protection for the worker and often create serious difficulties for the owners of private profit-making firms, and these difficulties may carry over into firms that are divested by the government. Details of the problems raised by restrictive labor codes are outlined in the subsequent discussion of the labor factor in privatization.

Fair treatment of the private sector under the tax code is important to entrepreneurial growth. Tax collection should be regularized and business made aware of the rules. These rules should be applied consistently and with as little change as possible over a period of time. Uncertainty as to possible tax rulings is a major obstacle to profitablility. It probably matters less what the tax rate is on a privatized firm than that the taxation is applied equably and consistently from year to year and to all taxpayers in a given category. The government must be persuaded that a confiscatory level of tax on profits will only serve to dry up the tax sources and that special tax favors (which are essentially hidden subsidies) applied in past to SOEs are no longer acceptable. Tax collectors may require additional training if new rulings are to be enforced, and higher standards of probity may have to be emphasized.

Modernization of the commercial code under which private business operates may be necessary as part of the privatization effort. Many former colonies continue to use commercial codes drawn up in the interest of trade with the mother country that are no longer applicable to an independent state. It is usually not necessary to replace the entire code; the Cote d'Ivoire, for example, still uses a code similar to that used in France, but with modifications and updating to meet the needs of a modern business community.

Ultimately, what will figure most prominently in foreign investor decisions are not only the code provisions but an overall investment climate that includes political stability, bureaucratic predictability, and legal clarity. Without these, governments are likely to find little buyer enthusiasm for their proposed divestments.

Human Impediments

The privatization process can be slowed down and even brought to a halt by the inexperience of those assigned to carry it out. Privatization is not simply a matter of offering an SOE for sale; it involves questions such as valuation, preparation of the offering, decisions on who should be allowed to bid, and negotiation for final disposal. Even the industrialized countries have found that government officers experienced in finance require special training for privatization. The need for such training is correspondingly greater in the case of LDC bureaucracies accustomed to working in relatively unsophisticated financial systems and with little contact with the private sector.

When faced with the complexities of a privatization, an official's tendency is often simply to delay the procedures indefinitely rather than admit ignorance of how to go about them. In some cases, the privatization assignment is simply one more task given to an already overburdened official so that it receives scant and belated attention, if any. Even if the specialized training in privatization techniques were available to them, many LDC governments could not spare employees for such training except at the cost of failing to accomplish pressing day-to-day tasks. The officials become, then, whether intentionally or by default, an impediment to rapid and efficient privatization. Many governments are aware of the problem and are making efforts to overcome it; in Malawi, for example, the Investment Coordinator's Office was specifically charged under a technical assistance contract with training Malawian civil servants in privatization procedures. Without their own trained officers, ministries are reluctantly forced to depend on external privatization specialists.

Privatization frequently involves the court system in decisions for which there is no precedent or provision in local legal codes. Judges have neither experience nor training on which to draw and, as with the bureaucracy, the result is inordinate delay in the judicial process. The court system may be heavily overloaded and court administration deficient to the point where a complex case never reaches the docket. Added to this is the ever present possibility of corruption of the judges or the lawyers involved in the case so that a fair hearing of the facts may become almost impossible. Almost any aspect of privatization may involve a legal contest, ranging from constitutional interpretation to argument between the buyer and the government over financial details. Given the weakness of many LDC court systems as a whole, combined with susceptibility of the judges to outside influence, the privatization process may face insuperable hurdles.

Improving Institutional Capabilities for Privatization

Although the overall institutional environment is important, successful privatization usually requires establishment of an office specifically designed to deal with details of the privatizing process; ministries or other government agencies are not normally geared to do so. Even if they were, privatizing is a full-time job, and civil servants are unable to devote their entire energies to it unless they are detailed to the task by specific direction.

The steps required in privatization are most expeditiously carried out if one high level official rather than a committee is made responsible. The "privatization czar" would be either a very senior civil servant (a permanent secretary, for example) or a political figure who has the full confidence of the leadership. It is highly desirable that the head of the privatization unit not only report to but have instant and continuous access to the president or the prime minister. Directives issued by the privatization chief should carry the authority of the highest level of government so that civil servants will be obliged to carry them out.

Those LDCs that have engaged in extensive privatization have usually created an institutional structure to oversee the process from the point of the decision to divest to the ultimate sale of the SOE. Some of these are headed by a minister; Canada opted for a minister for privatization, and in Togo the Ministry of State Enterprises was assigned the responsibility for privatizing. In Malawi the government appointed a Divestment Committee consisting of senior civil servants to make final recommendations to the Treasury on sales. This is usually less satisfactory, however, than a single dedicated individual whose sole function is privatization. Some privatization agencies include representatives of the private sector to ensure that its point of view is heard in the making of decisions and to maintain investor interest. Care should be taken, however, to avoid any apparent (if not real) conflict of interest in appointing such respresentatives.

Some members of the private sector may be potential buyers of the firms intended for divestment and hence should not be privy to discussion of the terms of sale.

The privatization agency, whatever its title, should be institutionalized as far as possible so that it has at least an air of permanency about it and should have staff and budget adequate to the task it is expected to perform. The particular form devised for the agency will differ with the circumstances and bureaucratic traditions of each country. Its powers may vary widely, depending on the degree to which the political leadership is prepared to delegate authority.

In some cases, authority to negotiate an entire privatization up to the point of sale is in the hands of the privatization secretariat, with oversight by a ministerial committee. In others, the government has mandated detailed procedures for choosing buyers (such as minimum prequalification to bid), limitations on acceptable bidders (such as ethnic qualifications), and requirements to guarantee public and transparent bidding arrangements. Although it may be desirable to specify careful prequalification conditions to ensure against frivolous bids, mandating procedures too closely has the effect of reducing the negotiating flexibility of the secretariat and hence its institutional usefulness.

If only a few small divestments are being made, they can be handled by a single official or minister with a small personal staff and some outside consultative assistance. In the case of a long-term privatization program dealing with larger SOEs, the privatization staff should become a recognized agency of the government. A wide variety of approaches has been taken by governments to institutionalize the privatization process. (Some of these examples are drawn from Vuylstekle, Nankani, and Candoy-Sekse, 1988, II).

- *Brazil.* An interministerial privatization council administers the entire procedure. It is chaired by the chief of the Planning Secretariat of the Presidency and is made up of the ministers of debureaucratization, finance, industry and trade, and the minister responsible for the SOE being privatized. It has an administrative secretariat but the leader in each case is the responsible sectoral ministry.

- *Malaysia.* An interdepartmental committee, chaired by the director of economic planning, has overall supervisory responsibility. The committee includes representatives of the Treasury, the Economic Planning Unit, and the Attorney General's Office.

- *The Philippines.* Oversight of the entire program rests in the hands of a Committee on Privatization which includes the minister of finance as chairman and also the secretary of the budget, secretary of government reorganization and trade, and secretary of industry, along with the director of the National Development Authority. Day-to-day responsibility for disposal of SOEs designated by the government lies in the hands of an Asset Privatization Trust whose members are appointed by the president.

- *Turkey.* Privatization procedures are defined by legislation passed in 1986. Decisions on the entities to be privatized is made by either the Council of Ministers or the Board of the Public Participation Fund (PPF), depending on the category of the enterprise. Once the decision is made, the firm automatically becomes a public company whose shares are transferred directly and without cost to the PPF.

   Previous legislation under which the SOE operated is overridden and all further decisions regarding management of the enterprise and the method of privatization are made by the fund. Dividends and proceeds of sales are channeled to the government by the PPF. The government has previously called on foreign and domestic investment banks to prepare overall privatization strategies. The Turkish system appears to have worked well, if the example of the highly successful privatization of part of the Posts and Telegraphs Agency early in 1988 is any indication.

- *Tunisia.* A two tier Commission structure on privatization actions has developed. A Technical Commission (CTAREP) assembles documentation on the financial and technical position of a firm and makes its recommendation to a higher body, the Commission for the Restructuring of Public Enterprises (CAREPP), made up of ministers and the chairman of the Central Bank. CAREPP in turn makes its recommendation to the Prime Minister who has the power of final decision. Tunisian institutions and procedures for privatization are discussed in detail in the case history on the Tunisian experience.

It also may be useful for the government to form an advisory or technical committee that may be called on when necessary by the privatization secretariat for help and that can also act as a buffer between the bureaucracy and the chief privatization official. The committee should include from the outset representatives of the private sector, possibly drawn from the financial community and chambers of commerce, as well as major interest groups, such as labor unions. In this way the government can minimize the accusation that it is acting in secret and provide an opportunity for a public information campaign directed to be by the secretariat.

Technical Assistance in Developing a Privatization Office

The array of expertise required by a privatization office will depend on the extent of the program envisaged. However, it is desirable that a central staff should be assembled that is sufficiently knowledgeable about all aspects of the privatization process so that it is able to judge the performance of outside expert consultants that may be required in highly technical fields. It is quite unlikely, in any case, that any government would have within its own bureaucracy all the specialized skills needed in privatization—ranging from financial experts, auditors, and legal counsel to specialists in manufacturing and marketing.

The services of local merchant bankers and other specialists, if they exist, may be brought in if special expertise on the local scene is needed. Malaysia, for example, used the services of a British investment firm that had played an important role in the privatization of British Telecoms, combined with those of a Kualalumpur investment bank, in privatizing Malaysian telecommunications and the national airlines. After two earlier privatizations, the Jamaican government had learned enough to be able to carry out the 1988 privatization of its telecommunications company virtually without outside advice.

In other instances, the most appropriate advice may be drawn from an internationally recognized investment banking firm with experience in privatization, particularly if the contemplated form of sale is a stock market offering. When the Guinean government recently embarked on privatization, an outside industrial investment firm was hired to carry out almost the entire procedure (analyzing SOEs to be sold, locating possible buyers, and advising the government during the subsequent negotiations). The role of government officials was minimal except in the final decisions, but it could not have reasonably been expected that Guinean civil servants had any prior experience in privatization.

External technical assistance can be very costly for the government unless it is provided by donor funds or an investment bank can be persuaded to undertake the job at less than in its normal fee (as in the case of the privatization of the National Commercial Bank in Jamaica) in the expectation that further business will result. However, it may be well worth the cost to the government in terms of institution building, if the contract with the foreign banking firm specifies that members of the privatization office work closely with the bank's staff or donor consultants throughout the entire procedure. The experience thus gained will make for an informed judgment on the work of experts hired for later privatizations and will provide enough knowledge so that staff members may need outside help only in the most highly specialized aspects of privatizing.

The privatization office is, of course, concerned with other aspects of privatization than just sale of SOEs. It may be required to deal with liquidation of a firm's assets only, partial privatization involving continued majority or minority government ownership, choice of management contractor if the decision should be made for continued ownership, and privatization of services. Dealing with these varied aspects of privatization with outside advice enhances the competence of the office to deal with the private sector and improves the government's overall relationship with business. Entrepreneurs are reassured by the knowledge that there is an established government agency that understands their problems and with which they can communicate.

The divestment and privatization of assets owned by the Agricultural Development and Marketing Corporation in Malawi provides a useful example of how technical assistance may be supplied. An experienced expatriate investment banker assumed responsibility for commissioning valuations of the firms, seeking buyers, conducting selling negotiations, and advising the senior officials sitting on the Divestment Committee on the best bids that met the criteria set by the government. In doing this he was assisted by special studies on financing that were carried out by a prominent British investment banking firm.

Skills Development as a Concomitant to Privatization

Privatization offers avenues for the development of specialized skills that would not otherwise be part of the training or experience of government officials or, indeed, anyone in the private sector. As the privatization program develops, the government may eventually be able to dispense with outside expertise.

While experts can be obtained through donor technical assistance programs, they are no substitute for government officers capable of evaluating advice given them by consultants. It is inevitable that an element of distrust, or at least of suspicion, will arise that some alternative privatization route may be more in the interest of the government than that recommended by the outside consultants. But there is no way of determining this if the privatization office staff is not in a position to know what alternatives exist.

The process of privatizing or rehabilitating SOEs for privatization should lead to the training of greater numbers of auditors and finance, valuation, and marketing specialists, to the benefit of both the government and the private sector. A further benefit will derive from the contacts that ministry officials will be able to make with international experts advising the privatization office. Familiarity with techniques of dealing with international donor agencies and potential multinational private sector buyers learned during privatization negotiations will gradually increase the confidence of government officials in their ability to argue the government's position effectively.

Of particular interest is the opportunity afforded the legal profession for specialized training in the legal intricacies of privatization. The assistance of local legal firms is important in the privatization process because they are more familiar with restrictions and limitations imposed by the country's laws and regulations. They can be especially helpful because of their knowledge of local political or family relationships upon which success of a privatization may depend.

In return, local lawyers are able to gain knowledge of a new legal field, which may include, for example, framing new legislation and regulations, especially in cases of joint ventures (the Republic of China, as a case in point, took several years to complete new joint venture regulations). Moreover, members of local law firms can gain direct experience in technical aspects of underwriting stock offerings or management contracting and leasing. The court system may be able to establish new precedents in ownership and property rights cases, as well as in legislative and constitutional interpretation.

Financing a privatization program will be of concern to the Treasury and to the banking system as a whole. Some institution building is likely in that both the Treasury and the banking system will be called upon by possible buyers to become familiar with financial instruments they have not dealt with before. For example, swapping of equity for debt, both internal and international, may be proposed as a method of financing the purchase of an SOE, and the government will have to be prepared to decide on a swapping policy and to negotiate the details of the deals. Local banks and brokers will probably need to work with an international adviser at the outset, but they can establish local investment banks as they gain experience. In Costa Rica, for example, a local financial group was eager to form such a bank with outside help to engage in privatization offerings.

Privatization by large stock offerings will usually require institutional strengthening of embryo stock markets by staff development and additional information systems. The Tunisian government, for example, contracted for a long-term consultant to develop a new regulative structure for the exchange and to train staff as part of a program of mobilizing financial markets for privatization. Foreign investors will increase the pressure to adopt internationally recognized accounting standards which may require additional training for local accountants.

Other financial instruments that will add strength to the institutional financing of privatization include:

• Liberalization of regulations to permit insurance companies and pension funds to buy shares in privatized state companies.

• Mutual funds or unit trusts that will hold shares in mixed SOEs and private firms, in which individual investors may buy shares.

• Government guaranteed convertible bonds, which may help to increase the number of issues in the stock market.

THE LABOR FACTOR IN PRIVATIZATION

As the number of privatizations increases worldwide, it has become evident that in many developing countries fear of opposition by labor leaders and the rank and file of trade unions is a major deterrent to more rapid progress in privatization efforts. The prospect that political unrest arising from unemployment may be a consequence of divestment has led many governments to approach privatizing very cautiously and has deterred some from embarking on it at all.

It is clear that any regime contemplating privatization must take the concerns of labor into account at every stage in the process. The government should be prepared to meet with labor leaders at an early point in discussion of the SOEs to be targeted for privatization, both to listen to labor's position and to reassure workers that their concerns are being taken seriously. Early demonstration by the government of the intention to make special efforts to avoid loss of jobs will reduce antagonism to privatization, particularly if it is accompanied by a well-planned educational campaign on the proposed methods of sale of the SOEs.

If unemployment is already severe under state management of the economy, the government will be doubly concerned about any action that threatens to produce further loss of jobs. On the other hand, in an absence of trade unions, as in Malawi, the unemployment question may not arise as a major factor in privatization. Labor reduction was not a matter of concern to the government in the sale of agricultural estates in part because much of the labor force is seasonal and the estates have a large labor pool on which to draw.

The Reality of the Unemployment Threat

Distrust of the private sector has been deep-seated for over a generation in most LDCs; business is stereotypically thought to be contrary to the interests of labor as a whole. Ideological opponents of private ownership can reinforce an already held popular prejudice to convince labor that sale of publicly owned means of production to private owners will only result in unemployment and exploitation of the workers.

Labor's immediate distrust of privatization is founded on a perception that it will inevitably be a threat to pensions and other labor rights and an awareness that SOEs are in most cases overmanned. Sale to the private sector will almost certainly result in reduction in the work force. But the widely accepted generalization that privatization will, in most cases, result in lower wages, deteriorated working conditions, and reduction in the labor force is subject to many exceptions and caveats that greatly reduce its validity both for the long and the short term.

The amount of reduction in the labor force depends to a large degree on its composition. Where the work force consists heavily of unskilled labor, there is a much greater chance of job loss, since productivity can be maintained or increased by giving greater incentives to fewer workers. On the other hand, the loss of jobs through privatization may be minimal where the labor force is composed largely of skilled workers whose services cannot be duplicated or dispensed with.

In the case of the National Bank of Jamaica, for example, privatization meant little or no loss of employment because most employees were trained in banking operations. There was little redundancy since the bank was well managed at the time of privatizing, and it could not operate without the skills of its present staff. To a large degree, the same situation applied in the case in Jamaica of the Caribbean Cement Company, whose operations were not labor intensive even before privatization.

In Turkey, the privatization of Teletas (the production arm of the telecommunications network) meant no serious staff losses because of the specialized skills of the workers. In Costa Rica, the proposed buyer of the national fertilizer company specified that, while it intended to move the location of the firm's research laboratory, all the scientists and technicians would be automatically retained if they were willing to move to the new site.

Many jobs in SOEs are, in fact, held by "phantom workers." What may be perceived to be a reduction in the work force may not be the case when phantom workers—who never appeared for work but were nevertheless paid—are removed. When combined with attrition through death, retirement, or job change, eliminating phantom workers may naturally reduce the work force without loss of any real jobs. The unions have less objection in such cases since they mean no actual reduction in dues-paying members employed by the firm.

Privatizing can be an instrument for increasing the work force over the long term. If a privatized firm is reorganized with new management and put on a profitable basis, it should be expected that its business will increase over time and that job opportunities and wages will also increase. Overall growth in the economy will follow with higher employment in other sectors, such as services that might not otherwise have been available.

Funds derived from the elimination of subsidies and the sale of divested SOEs may be applied to development projects producing new jobs. As a bridging mechanism, the government may have to create temporary job or retraining programs to prepare workers no longer required by privatized industries for new employment. These programs may absorb some of the revenues gained from privatization, but they will still be less costly than continued subsidy payments to money losing SOEs. The pressure to save jobs can be relieved if the government is prepared to find places for displaced workers in SOEs not yet scheduled for privatization, but this represents only a temporary alleviation of the problem.

The problem of unemployment is no more avoidable in rehabilitating SOEs than in privatizing them. Putting a firm on a profitable footing will require the same reduction in the work force, no matter who is the owner. Placing it under a management contract, even though the government remains the owner, may allow the government some voice in employee layoffs, but if the government seeks to interfere too strongly with the manager's hiring and firing prerogatives (normally a condition of management contracts), the terms of the contract may be abrogated. If the government's major objective is profitability, short-term unemployment during rehabilitation may be the price that has to be paid.

The Dynamics of Management/Labor/Government Relations in Privatization

In order to successfully involve all parties, the dynamics of a privatization must be integrated with the concerns of labor, the private sector buyer, and the government. Insofar as labor issues are concerned, there are essentially five interested parties in any privatization process:

1. *The rank and file of the work force*, whether organized into unions or not. Apart from the actual loss of employment, they are concerned with the relationship between wage scales in the public and the private sector, pensions, seniority rights, and other perquisites.

2. *The leaders of organized labor*, who are concerned with the preservation of their own power and prestige, which are based ultimately on membership strength and solidarity. Reduced membership as a result of layoffs will inevitably undermine the position of union heads. It may be possible to persuade the labor leadership to take at least a wait-and-see attitude toward initial privatizations before raising objection by including restrictions on reducing the labor force for a given period after the sale.

3. *The managers of firms being privatized*, who have both a labor and a management interest. New private owners may seek to replace the entire management team of the former SOE or at least individual members of it. Many SOEs suffer as much from overmanning at the managerial level as they do at the worker level, and managers are per capita more costly. Privatization not only threatens managers with loss of their own jobs. Even those who are retained may face job insecurity or a recalcitrant labor force. As a result, management may be as strongly opposed to privatization as is labor, although it is likely to be less vocal in its protest.

4. *The government as the seller of the SOE*. Most governments cannot afford to alienate the important segment of the voters represented by labor, whatever the form of the

regime. In an elective system, the government may well depend for a significant part of its support on organized labor, especially in those countries in which political interest group organization is only at the rudimentary stage. Withdrawal of union support over the issue of privatization could mean defeat of the governing party.

5. *The prospective buyer*, whether individual or shareholder. The position of labor may be critical to the decision to buy a privatized firm. If trade unions adamantly oppose privatization, they will continue to be a source of problems to the buyers when the buyers later seek to reduce the labor force. The possibility of an indefinite period of strikes, slowdowns, and protests that would interrupt production, as would delays caused by labor retraining, greatly diminishes the interest of prospective buyers. Similarly, the burden of high levels of pensions or other workers' rights that may have to be assumed by the buyers could reduce the firm's potential profit levels to the point at which ownership is not worthwhile.

In addition to considering the interests of these various parties, the government faces other constraints in dealing with organized labor. In planning privatization, the government will have to be aware of the social and financial costs involved in divesting, as well as its own interests as an employer and as a recipient of labor's political support. In many developing countries, SOEs have taken the place of a social security system. The government, as the employer, provides the worker not only with wages but the only available retirement support, unemployment compensation, some contribution to health insurance, and in many instances, housing. A private employer is unlikely to provide all of these perquisites (unless required to as a condition of sale) and the government will have to find some means of replacing them.

In privatization planning, the provisions of the labor code have implications for both the workers and the potential purchaser of an SOE. The labor code has often acted as an inhibiting factor in the sale of SOEs in developing countries, no matter how well the privatization strategy has been planned. Potential buyers are interested in freedom to hire and fire, the skill level of available new employees and, within limits, freedom from government interference in setting wages (a universal minimum wage law, for example, would not be considered such interference). Some LDC governments may seek to limit the number of expatriates that may be employed in management or technical positions or the length of time any one expatriate may remain in the post without indigenous replacement. Expatriate managers may be subject to local political pressures to hire certain individuals or numbers of employees. In some countries, such as Panama, labor code provisions applying to SOEs and to private sector firms may differ. In others, provisions may also differ for SOEs created by the government from those applied to existing firms that have been nationalized.

Codes drawn up in the first years after the independence of former colonies were often heavily weighted in favor of labor, partially as a result of the reaction against expatriate colonial employers and partially because of the heavy influence of socialist doctrines. After two decades, however, as it has become more evident that these restrictive codes have constituted a deterrent to much needed foreign investment, many governments are now seeking a balance between labor and employer interests.

New liberalized codes in some African countries, for example, allow greater latitude to the employer in making labor decisions affecting the profitability of the firm (such as in hiring and firing and setting of wage rates) while the code prescribes general guidelines for overtime, vacation, and working conditions. Several of the latest codes give incentives to foreign employers to provide training programs for workers that result in transfer of technological skills. Although employee rights are still prominently featured, grievance procedures have been simplified to make for more prompt settlement with less loss of production time.

Accumulated pension rights provide one of the most serious roadblocks to privatization sales. Most SOE pension funds are not vested, relying on the government to provide funds as needed. Investors considering purchase of major SOEs have balked at assuming the accumulated costs of pensions and other rights, forcing the government either to assume this burden as part of the sales agreement or substantially reduce the price of the firm being sold. It is to the government's advantage, then, to eliminate major inequities by rewriting the labor code prior to privatization, but this may not be possible in the face of determined union opposition.

Overcoming Labor's Objections to Privatization

A variety of methods is available to reduce labor's legitimate fears of the consequences of privatizing large SOEs. Each method has to be adapted, however, to the particular circumstances of the enterprises themselves and to the state of the national economy as a whole. If an economy is in a period of growth, alternative job opportunities may be readily available so that the effect of privatization will scarcely be felt. This is more likely to be the case in an already industrialized economy. For example, after an initial drop, employment in the privatized British Airways increased as the company's business improved under private management.

But in the developing world it is much more often the case that the government is seeking to reduce financial pressures by privatizing because the economy is in a state of stagnation or even of decline. Unemployment rates are often highest among the young school-leavers with high job expectations; this group is the most politically sensitized and therefore most vocal in its demands. Failure to make entry-level job opportunities available can undermine the value attached to education as well as constituting a serious political threat to the government.

The level of public anxiety accompanying large-scale privatizations can be lowered by a general education campaign on the meaning of the term and on the implications of privatizing for the society as a whole. Part of this campaign can be directed specifically to answering the doubts and fears of labor.

A well-planned and well-executed educational campaign on the meaning of privatization can pay off handsomely through an increase in labor's acceptance of the government's plans. Ignorance of the steps involved (valuation, marketing, financing, etc.) in selling enterprises owned and run by the state is to be expected, especially in countries in which state management of the economy has been pervasive. The government's own motives for privatizing should be publicly exposed, pointing up the long-range advantages to privatization while not glossing over the short-range problems it will create. The government's explanations must be (and must be perceived to be) honest and straightforward; any attempt to conceal the intention of the political leaders will only harden labor's attitude and reinforce the negative perception of privatization. If the government is considering labor participation in sale of stock, the conditions, as well as the meaning of stock ownership, should be clarified in detail.

The government should make special efforts to see that labor objections are specifically addressed in any educational campaign. In the case of the National Commercial Bank in Jamaica, the government not only provided public information but also invited labor leaders to private meetings at the highest levels of government prior to announcing a final decision to privatize. In these gatherings, in order to ensure that the government had an opportunity to hear the labor viewpoint, specific concerns about pensions, worker rights, and unemployment were addressed in as much detail as possible.

Part of the goal of listening to, and providing concrete answers for, labor's questions is to preempt initiation of an opposition campaign by organized labor before the privatization strategy is announced. It should be made clear to union leaders that continued public ownership of a firm is no guarantee that current rates of employment will prevail. If economic conditions prevent further subsidy payments, the firm will ultimately be forced out of business with a consequent loss of all jobs. From labor's viewpoint, ownership is not as important as profitability of the firm; making a profit is one of the best ways to ensure stable levels of employment in either the public or the private sector.

Planning for Employment of Redundant Workers

In the industrialized countries, experience thus far has shown that labor's fear that privatization will lead to job losses is generally justified since overemployment is chronic in state-owned enterprises. In countries where multiple industrial opportunities exist, placement of surplus labor may not be a problem, although some retraining may be required. Facilities to deal with the problem, such as labor exchanges, are already established, and social insurance is available for the unemployed.

In developing countries, however, where unemployment rates, particularly in urban areas, are high and there is little alternative industrial employment and no social security system, the government will be particularly cautious in privatizing large labor-intensive industries. The cost of removing substantial numbers of people from existing jobs in the interests of efficiency and higher productivity can be high, both financially and politically. Immediate financial costs involving severance pay, pensions, and other benefits as well as retraining programs must be balanced against the benefits of relief from subsidy payments and long-term gains in economic growth.

Privatization may eventually increase employment as a result of new product lines or more efficient management of the privatized firms, but it will still mean an initial loss of jobs. Even in industrialized countries this cannot be avoided. Privatizing Japanese National Railways, for example, meant a loss of ninety-two thousand jobs. In France, the sale of the Compagnie Générale de Constructions Téléphoniques brought about the eventual loss of one quarter of the work force, even though the buyer was initially required by the labor code to absorb all employees (Vuylsteke, Nankani and Candoy-Sekse, 1988, I:129-30). In LDCs that have used SOEs to serve social as well as economic ends, employee layoffs could have very serious consequences.

If the government feels politically strong enough to resist the pressure, it can simply ignore worker objections to layoffs. In Ghana, for example, drastic action was taken to reduce the 100,000 employees of the Cocoa Marketing Board as part of the government's target to reduce the civil service by 5 percent annually. Some twenty-five thousand phantom employees were eliminated and fifteen thousand others laid off. The Ghanaian action was made possible by the fact that it was done under a military regime; under other circumstances a more gradual and phased reduction would probably have been necessary to preserve the government.

It is possible, of course, to leave the whole problem in the hands of the new owners, who will reduce staff to meet their needs and hope that the situation will be accepted by labor. But this has a substantial element of risk. If the buyers are going to have to shoulder the costs of dismissal of workers and post-sale labor agitation, the price they will be prepared to pay for the firm may be unacceptable. The government may have to seriously consider whether it is preferable to protect retirement and separation benefits or attempt to preserve or create new jobs for displaced workers.

Another option is to make specific provisions for redundant workers. If the government's plans to employ laid off workers are made public before putting any state-owned firms on the market, labor resistance may be reduced. Announcement of plans to deal with unemployment may also forestall legal action by trade unions seeking to prevent the government from embarking on any privatization at all. Should the unions feel that their only recourse to prevent privatizing is to seek court injunction against it, all privatization action could be held up indefinitely, even if the union's case were ultimately lost. If the charge is illegal sale of public goods or unconstitutional abrogation of workers' rights, the case could be both long and costly.

Should the process become too prolonged, the regime may change, or the government may decide that, if there is strong public support for the unions' position, privatization is too risky and the whole effort may be dropped. Avoiding court action is in everyone's interest. In the end, the government stands to be the greater loser if it is forced to back down.

The government can show its concern for labor's position by providing new jobs for redundant workers in other SOEs. Tunisia, for example, created jobs for workers in privatized or liquidated firms through what was essentially a public works program, implemented to tide workers over for a temporary period while they sought reentry into the labor market. In some cases (Sri Lanka, for example) part of the proceeds of sales of SOEs has been set aside for severance pay; in the Sudan and Mali, special funds (in the case of Mali, with outside donor assistance) were set up to provide loans to workers to permit them to go into business for themselves.

There are cases, as in Guinea, where the government has retained in civil service positions workers of privatized firms who have been unable to find jobs in the private sector. This guaranteed employment may minimize the objection to privatizing but in the end does little to reduce the number of government employees. It may also be possible to create a special pool of former workers in privatized firms who would receive preferential placement in jobs for which they qualify. If accusations of favoritism in placement can be avoided, this may serve as a public demonstration of government's concern for displaced labor.

An obvious remedy for reducing labor's anxieties is to create retraining programs for redundant workers, if the government and the new private owner can agree at the time of sale on the number of surplus workers that will be created. The problem with retraining, however, is that careful prior planning is required so that the workers are retrained for jobs for which there is some prospective need. All too often the tendency is to train for jobs already in surplus simply because the training facilities and personnel are available. Little purpose will be served, however, if the government fails to provide job placement services at the conclusion of the retraining.

Despite all the government's best efforts to cut back the human cost of privatizing, labor's fears may be sufficiently deep-rooted that privatization of larger enterprises will never be accepted. If this is the case, the government may be well advised to concentrate on smaller firms until a track record can be set that will offer proof that the government's announced plans to ensure minimal unemployment are, in fact, effective.

Apart from continued employment, one of labor's major concerns is the preservation of workers' pension and seniority rights within the privatized firm or in employment in other private sector firms. Employees of SOEs are often considered to be civil servants for purposes of pension and accumulate rights based on civil service standards that are frequently more generous than those in the private sector. Such employees may be given the option of remaining in this system or joining the private pension structure of the new employer without loss of retirement pay. The private employer may offer additional incentives such as longer vacations and health or other benefits. A third option may be to offer a generous lump sum redundancy settlement or severance bonus with early retirement. Although none of these represents the perfect solution to protecting employee interests at reasonable cost to the government, some combination of them may be necessary to prevent labor unrest. Examples of application of some of these alternatives in dealing with the problem of redundant workers can be found in Malaysia, Bangladesh, Panama, and Peru.

Malaysia. One of the most specific policies formulated to provide for the transition of workers from public to private industries is found in the *Guidelines on Privatization*, issued by the Malaysian government. These guidelines provide that all employees in privatized firms must not lose any benefits they previously enjoyed under public employment. It is made clear to all prospective buyers that this policy applies to the purchase of any SOE, and it becomes a requirement of ownership. Detailed employment provisions of the policy require that:

New owners accept all employees who choose to stay with the firm. No workers may be laid off (except for disciplinary reasons) for five years. Should the worker opt not to join the new company, he must retire (if he is old enough) or simply resign. In the case of two major privatizations, 99 percent of the former SOE employees opted to join the new company. Available data do not indicate what effect these obligations had on the sale price of the SOE.

Employment benefits were a matter of employee choice. The new companies offered schemes that included provisions for bonuses and share ownership which made for higher take home pay but less job security. Alternatively, employees could opt to remain within the government's civil service scheme which gave them government paid subsidized housing and car loans, although their wages were paid by the new private employer. This meant better fringe benefits and greater employment security but lower take home pay. For employees choosing this option, the employer continued to pay directly into the government pension fund for them. (Vuylsteke, Nankani, and Candoy-Sekse, 1988, II:67–69.)

Bangladesh. When the nationalized Bangladesh jute mills were returned to private ownership in 1985, the conditions of sale required the new owners to retain all current employees for a period of twelve months, after which the employers were, in theory, free to reduce staff as they saw fit. However, as Lorch (1988:33) points out, in practice it was extremely difficult to dismiss workers because of high severance pay requirements (three to five monthly wage payments plus one month for every year of employment) and labor opposition. Some employers decided to resolve the entire problem by paying surplus employees twelve months wages at the time of purchase.

The organized urban industrial work force was strongly (and even violently) opposed to privatization from the beginning. A general strike was called against the government's privatization policies in April 1987 and Divestment Resistance Committees were created (Humphrey, 1988:112). Strikes and demonstrations that involved kidnapping of factory managers were common occurrences at this period, and the government appeared almost powerless to control them. Labor pressure forced the government to reaffirm its continued support for SOEs and to relax its protection of factory owners against labor violence. The privatized mills were required to meet the wage and benefit levels of state enterprises.

It is very difficult to secure any accurate estimate of the reduction in employment as a result of privatization in jute mills. Figures range from 1.4 percent to 10 percent, depending on their source and whether phantom workers (whose wages were pocketed by managers) are counted. Early retirements and attrition provided some relief. Redundancy was as much a problem with managers as with the labor force, and it was easier to reduce their numbers by using the "golden handshake." On the other hand, the increased business in some privatized textile mills caused a rise in employment of as much as 20 percent.

Jute mill owners were also able to reduce labor costs by eliminating supervisory personnel, substituting unskilled for skilled workers, and changing laborers' status from regular to casual employment that did not require payment of benefits. In a country like Bangladesh where urban unemployment is chronic, however, it is unlikely that further substantial reductions can be made in labor costs in the face of continued union opposition.

Panama. As is the case with other Central American countries, Panama imposes such severe burdens on the employer through its labor code that it virtually prevents a private buyer from acquiring a state-owned enterprise through privatization unless prior detailed decisions are taken to resolve personnel questions. Any attempt to reduce the labor force in the overmanned Panamanian SOEs invokes highly complex severance and benefit liabilities and certain established practices and acquired rights, as well as contracts calling for higher wages than are normal in the private sector. A further complication is that SOEs are divided between those that come under the labor code and those that come under the administrative code. Each code carries differing implications for the treatment of surplus labor.

A group of SOEs (consisting chiefly of firms that were once private but later taken over by the government) are considered private stock corporations subject to the labor code. Those firms are subject to extremely rigid limitations on firing and substantial benefits are accrued for dismissal. Employees may contest dismissal with a final decision coming only after lengthy judicial procedures. For employees with ten years or more of service, the cost to the firm of dismissal, even for justified reasons, can be very high. A firm being privatized with 250 surplus employees, for example, might pay as much as $2 million in accumulated labor liabilities. Severance pay and seniority bonuses are so substantial that most firms of any size have established funded contingency reserves to meet these demands. As a result of the code provisions, any prospective buyer of this category of firm would require assumption by the government of all labor liabilities as a prerequisite to serious negotiation.

Firms established by the government (denoted as parastatals) fall under the administrative code governing civil service employment. They require no justification for firing and no benefits accrue. The purchaser of a firm under the administrative code is not regarded from a legal point of view as buying an existing corporation, but rather buying purely assets. Employees under the administrative code retained by the new company created by a privatization would thereupon come under the labor code and would begin a new contractual relationship with no previous accumulation of benefits.

It has been proposed that the most expeditious and economic way to handle privatization of a Panamanian firm under the labor code would be to secure from all employees a voluntary resignation, after having negotiated with them financial incentives greater than what would have been obtained under the "unjustified dismissal" terms of the labor code. These negotiations would have to be carried out by the government. A similar negotiation could be held with employees under the administrative code, offering them a bonus for resignation prior to privatizing.

Successful completion of the negotiations would make the sale of the firm much easier and would reduce political complications for the government. The new buyer would be under no obligation to take on any employees of the former SOE.

Prior to the recent internal political and economic upheaval in Panama, there appeared to be general agreement on the formation of a severance pay fund. If the current situation changes, it is not clear whether the trade unions will agree to such a fund if they feel that their political power is being reduced by loss of membership. Employee reaction will depend on the generosity of the offer made by the government.

Peru. The inspiration for the proposed Panamanian program was drawn in part from the Peruvian employee buy-out experience. Faced with a labor code having essentially the same provisions as that in Panama, the government embarked as early as 1983 on a program of buy-outs that permitted full and partial privatizations. Privatization of a tuna cannery was accomplished through the resignation of all 1,800 employees in the state-owned factory after payment of a bonus to the workers. Similarly, a bonus was utilized by a fishmeal plant to reduce its labor force to 4,500 from 6,000 employees, to enable partial privatization, and by a fish marketing firm, to cut its labor force in half. As early as 1978, the government had pointed the way by cutting its own labor force by 2 percent through offering a bonus of eight months salary.

Bonus buy-out programs, no matter what form they take, are relatively expensive for the government. However, if the cost of annual subsidy to a money losing SOE is compared with the one-time cost of a bonus buy-out enabling the government to free itself from subsidy payments by privatizing, the latter is clearly to the government's advantage. In the case of the Peruvian fishmeal plant, the bonus program cost $24 million; the annual subsidy to keep the plant operating was $35 million.

Encouraging Employee Participation in Privatized Enterprises

One recently developed method of meeting labor's retrenchment concerns is to provide the opportunity for employees to become part or full owners of the firm being privatized through a preferred stock offering, labor/management buyout, or employee stock ownership program (ESOP). The assumption behind these methods is that if employees become the new owners, much of their objection to divestment will fall away. As owners, they will share in the profits to be made by the privatized firm, have a substantial share in management decisions, and enjoy greater job security if the firm prospers as a result of greater worker productivity. From the government's point of view, a sale with employee participation gives public evidence of official concern for fair treatment of the worker, reduces the need to deal with the surplus labor question, and obviates the political charge that the privatization program is a vehicle to enrich foreign or special domestic interests.

Structuring an employee participation program can, however, be costly both in time and money, and the plan may not always be popular with a firm's labor force. Its advantages must be clearly explained, particularly in situations where workers are not familiar with owning shares of stock and for whom investment extends little beyond the concept of real property.

Employee Stock Offering Schemes

Once those eligible are aware of the possibility of returns both in dividends and capital appreciation from share ownership, most employee stock offerings have been oversubscribed. A wide variety of incentives has been used to raise employee interest. For example, a specific percentage of the offering is reserved for employees (usually between 5 and 10 percent). Shares are made available at a discount from the offering price ranging from 5 percent at the time of sale to 20 percent if the shares are held for at least two years. In many cases, special loan arrangements are made at low rates for employee purchases, or payment may be arranged over one or two years through direct withdrawals from wages. Limits for individual employee purchases are often set, at least in the first offering period. Any remaining shares are then offered first to employees at the full offering price.

Another incentive is an outright gift of shares or free shares tied to purchases of additional shares. While this may be a denial of free market considerations and cost the government some revenue in the short term, it may encourage organized labor to support later privatizations. If the free shares have gone up in value, the public may be encouraged to buy at full price next time an offering is put on the market. An additional incentive may be built into the initial offering price by setting it below market value with the certainty that the shares will show an immediate profit, thus encouraging purchases when the next offer comes on the market.

A combination of these incentives was used, for example, in the marketing of the National Bank of Jamaica stock. Employees were offered 20 free shares, up to 350 matching shares at the offering price, 850 shares at 10 percent discount, and a further 850 priority shares at the offering price. Payment could be made over two years through salary deduction. Similar arrangements were made for employee purchase in the case of Teletas in Turkey. It has also been commonly used in major privatizations in France and the United Kingdom, with conspicuous success.

The point is sometimes made that in many developing countries, employees do not have the capital available to buy stock. This would not appear to hold true for offerings in the more advanced developing countries, where demand has outstripped supply at the discounted price. With a stock offering, employees do not have a controlling interest in the firm, but they do have a substantial stake in its future.

The Labor/Management Buy-Out

In a labor/management buy-out, a combination of labor and management gains a controlling interest in the firm being privatized, often by means of leveraging. Several examples of this are to be found in recent British privatizations, the best known of which is the National Freight Company. A management and labor group bought the company with combination of a loan and employee equity subscription purchased by 80 percent of the employees. They were rewarded with a substantial increase in share value in a very short time. Other examples include a water supply company in the Cote d'Ivoire that was taken over in a buy-out to avoid liquidation and a number of buy-outs with full or partial worker participation in Chile. A problem of such labor/management buy-outs is that if the firm fails to generate profits because of heavy initial debt service costs, worker/shareholders may sell their stock at low rates to investors to avoid losses. Control of the firm could then pass to a few individuals who might profit handsomely when and if the firm can be turned around.

The limited number of labor/management buy-outs that have occurred in the developing world is insufficient to judge their usefulness as an instrument for preserving jobs in privatization. They may be attempted if enough credit facilities to acquire the firm are available, but workers investing their limited capital should be aware of the element of risk in the undertaking.

Employee Stock Ownership Plans (ESOPs)

Employee stock ownership plans are basically a financing technique that permits employees of a firm to acquire ownership of all or part of the firm's stock without personal investment on their part. The stock may be a new issue or a transfer of existing assets, such as would take place in a privatization. An ESOP fund is created by borrowing from banks, and the fund is used to acquire the company's stock. Each employee participant receives an allocation of stock to a personal account, and as the ESOP loan is repaid (by employer contribution to the plan), the plan's trustees allocate to each employee his share of the total.

ESOPs have up to now been a peculiarly American initiative because of the tax advantages afforded by U.S. legislation. Among others, these include:

• An annual contribution paid by the employer to each employee's ESOP account up to 25 percent of pay. This may be deducted against corporate income tax.

• In the case of an ESOP loan, the company can claim an income tax deduction for both principal and interest paid, since these are treated as business expenses for the funding of an employee benefit plan.

• The individual ESOP stockholder may, under certain circumstances, defer taxes on profits of stock sold back to the ESOP.

• Fifty percent of the proceeds realized from the sale of the firm's stock to an ESOP are excluded from estate tax.

Tax reductions, both individual and corporate, provide powerful incentives for the formation of ESOPs in the United States, but they are not usually found in foreign tax systems. It has been argued that it is the ESOP concept that is important; adapting it to the conditions in developing countries will require imagination and flexibility in changing the tax structure. Although ESOPs are a relatively advanced concept for developing countries, requiring both legal skills and acceptance of share ownership, they may have application where a comparatively sophisticated financial system is in place. It is unlikely, however, that they will become a common method of saving employees from job loss as a result of privatization.

A CONCLUDING NOTE—MAKING THE PRIVATIZATION STRATEGY WORK

It cannot be emphasized too strongly that the decision to privatize is in the first instance political, regardless of the economic and financial pressures that may have prompted consideration of the move. Virtually every facet of the privatizing process has its political overtone, ranging from deciding what to privatize and how to privatize it to choosing the buyer and in some cases finding financing for the deal. By deciding to divest SOEs, the government is taking a political risk that could range from alienating a few high level supporters to popular discontent that might overthrow the regime. If the benefits from privatizing do not become evident within a reasonable period in the form of more and cheaper consumer goods or increasing income, the government may be tempted to give up the entire project.

Outside technical advice on reducing political risk may be helpful, but only if those giving it are sufficiently well acquainted with the political environment and the government's objectives to suggest effective actions that are still within the bounds of the politically possible. Because of the high degree of sensitivity involved, the public perception must be avoided that privatization is being managed or directed from the outside, or that it is being pushed in by foreign ideology or interest. Reducing political obstacles is a matter of the government's judgment alone; the most an outsider can do is play a low key role, giving advice only when asked.

In any estimate of the chances for successful privatization, the financial and social conditions in which the privatization is taking place must be taken into account at every stage of the strategy. The more sophisticated the financial structure of the country, the easier privatization will be. If the government is committed to a policy of broad redistribution of wealth as part of its social program, the existence of an established capital market will help to create greater public acceptance of a sale by stock offering. Sale of shares through a unit trust or mutual fund can add substantially to the numbers of those familiar with investment as a form of saving and thus to the modernization of the society as a whole.

Full prior consideration by the government of the institutional consequences of privatizing are critical to the success of strategic planning for the campaign. While this is in some degree generic to privatization whether in industrialized or developing countries, it is of special importance in LDCs where the institutional structures are still in the process of change and the capabilities of the government's regulatory powers are not yet fully utilized. It cannot be expected that all the institutional changes needed to facilitate privatization will be accomplished before divestment begins. But hesitation on the part of potential buyers can be reduced if the government offers firm evidence that institutional reform is high on its agenda. Strong labor opposition to privatization, particularly if it is allied with the government's political opponents, can prevent divestment of large labor-intensive SOEs if the government is not decisive in handling questions of pension rights and labor code reforms.

The impediments created by opposition forces are not insurmountable if the government is firm in its determination to divest and has the political will to push through its privatization plan. But early planning on how to deal with these impediments when they arise will avoid crises that could seriously interrupt current privatization actions once the strategic plan is implemented.

It is at the level of institutional change that outside donor assistance can play an especially important role. Technical assistance leading to regulatory change not only makes privatization easier but can also assist private sector development generally. Policy dialogue focused on eliminating obstacles to free market operation and financial development are indirectly supportive of the privatization program, as is encouragement of competition to SOEs by donor help with new private sector inititatives.

3

The Techniques of Privatization—Implementing a Divestment Plan

INTRODUCTION

In many LDCs, making a policy decision is often confused with carrying out the policy. Once having decided to embark on privatization and having developed an outline of strategy, the government may have the tendency to assume that the task has automatically been accomplished. Implementation, however, of the privatization plan is the next and most crucial step. Several different issues must be addressed at the outset:

- Which firms should be selected for privatization?

- What must be done to prepare the firms proposed for divestment in order to offer them for sale?

- What techniques and instruments are to be used to sell the firms?

- To whom will the firms be sold, either as units to individual investors or as equity investments to shareholders? What buyers are acceptable and to what extent is foreign investment, either direct or in joint venture, politically acceptable?

- How are the privatizations to be financed?

- Does the government contemplate complete divestment of the SOEs or does it seek to maintain an equity interest in the divested firms (i.e., partial divestment)? If the latter option is chosen, how does the government protect its public policy interests if it becomes, in effect, a minority shareholder?

- For those SOEs that are in such poor financial shape that they are unlikely to attract buyers but which have potential for profitable operation, is the government prepared to engage in a program of rationalization to bring them to a point at which a private investor may be interested?

The government should be aware of the close relationship between the objectives it may have set in developing the privatization strategy and the techniques that are used for implementation. If, for example, one objective is wide distribution of ownership, sale of shares to the general public is an obvious instrument, although it may entail higher marketing costs than would sale to an individual buyer. The trade-off is distribution of wealth to the public, to specific ethnic groups, or to the employees of the divested companies versus maximizing the net sale profits. No instrument is without its political or economic costs.

CHOOSING THE CANDIDATES FOR DIVESTMENT

The correct choice of the assets initially to be divested and the order in which others will follow may be crucial to the success of the entire privatization plan. Some countries, such as Guinea, made the decision to work on all fronts at once—the industrial, financial, agricultural, and service sectors. Others, depending on local circumstances, have been more selective, placing early emphasis on those SOEs requiring the heaviest subsidies or those that are judged to be the most marketable. A few privatization plans have given early priority to the service or the agricultural sectors. A variety of factors can play a role in the choice.

If the government's goal is the largest possible addition to revenue, privatization will be started with those units that offer prospect of sale at the highest price. Firms that show current profitability will be the most marketable. In order to demonstrate that state enterprises can be sold, there may be advantages to disposing of these at the beginning. The next stage will be to try to sell those that are not currently profitable but which, if better managed in private hands, may become so. This strategy was employed, for example, in Grenada.

The size of the firms being put on the market may be a determinant. Successful privatization of large service industries, such as telecommunications, electrical generating firms, or transportation services, is clearly in the government's interest because they will produce the highest prices while at the same time reducing subsidy costs. Successful sale of broadly used public services will help to create popular support for privatization generally over the long term if service to the consumer is clearly improved immediately after the divestment. But beginning the privatization venture with these units poses serious problems. It may be extremely difficult to find a single buyer because of the heavy capitalization involved. The government may need to spin off some parts of the assets to break down the sale into manageable portions. Moreover, in most LDCs these assets are frequently the largest money losers and are, therefore, the least attractive to the private sector. Finding a suitable buyer may involve sale to foreign interests which, because of the importance of these services to national security, the government may be reluctant to countenance. Failure to find a single buyer or a consortium because the sale is too large for the local market to absorb may create an adverse public impression of the privatization program, thereby providing an excuse for the government to abandon the entire effort.

If a stock flotation is planned as the mechanism of divestment, the cost of expert advice from investment bankers will be high. On the other hand, an investment bank experienced in privatization hired to manage the flotation may be able to sell the stock for a higher return than would be received from a private placement.

Privatization of firms or services that are large employers will usually mean large reductions in the work force, creating greater opportunity for labor objection. Starting the program with privatization of smaller SOEs will be less complicated and can be carried out with greater speed. Local buyers are more apt to come forward, costly expert advice will not be necessary, and employee redundancy will be greatly reduced. But this approach too has real disadvantages.

When a large unit is privatized, the government gets the credit, and if a stock market flotation is used, public awareness rises sharply when several thousand new shareholders are created. The Malaysian plan to privatize the telecommunications system received wide publicity both at home and abroad, while in Grenada the sale of several small SOEs involving only a few dozen employees went largely unnoticed.

The optimum choice would appear to lie midway between large and small assets. Ideally, the first privatization would be of a substantial and well-known enterprise whose product or service is easily recognized in the local market, preferably a successful SOE that has not required subsidy and has been operated by an efficient, business-like management. Such a candidate may generate sufficient buyer interest to allow the government to choose from among the highest bidders. Unfortunately, a firm meeting these conditions is unlikely to be among those to be privatized first, even though it may represent the best way to create support for further privatization, since it is a revenue producer for the government.

Whatever alternative is chosen, the selection remains a crucial element to the success of the government's long-range strategy. Factors such as the strength of the local capital market and the pressures that opponents of privatization can bring to bear before the first privatization is announced should be carefully weighed. Once the list of candidates is decided upon, the offering should remain open for a reasonable period of time; too protracted a period, however, will serve to diminish the value of the asset as well as buyer interest.

As the Tunisian case illustrates, releasing the list of firms to be privatized in advance of any action by the privatization secretariat poses problems. Managers of firms not on the published list may feel that they are secure and under no pressure to make changes that might lead to greater efficiency and, therefore, profitability. It is preferable simply to announce that all SOEs are being considered for privatization (whether or not this may actually be the case) so that managers will be alerted that their firms may be put on the block at any time.

PREPARING AN SOE FOR SALE

The great majority of SOEs cannot be simply placed on the market without substantial preparation. Potential buyers will seek detailed information on the condition of the firm that will require some time to assemble and can often best be put together by outside accountants and investment bankers.

A basic analysis starts with the question of whether or not the firm is currently profitable, is potentially profitable, or is essentially a business that cannot be made to produce a profit and, therefore, should be liquidated. Even revenue producing SOEs might be made more profitable in private hands, and the government could thereby increase its revenues by taxation. Currently unprofitable firms could be rehabilitated and later sold, but this involves further capital investment that the government may be unwilling or unable to undertake. Liquidation is the most unpalatable solution since it means writing off much of the previous investment.

Detailed analysis of a firm may reveal that one particular privatization instrument is more suitable than any other, given the nature of the business and the firm's operating experience. This analysis should include at least the following major elements:

1. Financial Performance
   - Knowledge of current balance sheets, debt-equity ratio, debt status, and corporate financial history.
   - Profit or loss on individual product lines. This should be analyzed with and without subsidy since the product may not be viable without subsidy.
   - Sources of capital funding and current working capital status as well as rate and commitment of capital expenditure. Terms and restrictions of borrowing powers of the firm should be considered—can capital be secured only from government allocation or also from domestic lenders and foreign investors?
   - Auditing procedures, efficiency of billing and disbursement practices, effectiveness of cost accounting (if any), and overall cash-flow dimensions. Overall financial performance may be compared to industry standards in other countries.

2. Technology and Productivity of the Firm

   Appropriateness of technology used, utilization of machinery and labor, performance of operations and scheduling of production. Is the technology outdated? If so what capital investment is needed to bring it up to industry standards and what improvements would be necessary in labor training?

3. Pricing Policies

   SOEs are frequently subject to price distortions of their products by government controlled prices and availability of subsidies. Information is necessary on how prices are set, by whom and through what procedures. What should be the "real" prices as opposed to those made possible by import restrictions and subsidies? Has research been done on price responsiveness of the market? Could the firm survive if it were exposed to competitive local market forces in product pricing?

4. Current and Past Marketing Strategies

   The failure to develop a marketing strategy has often been a strong contributing factor to the failure of SOEs. Since they are not in a competitive market, too little attention has been paid to sales and to adjustment of product lines to consumer demand. In the case of state enterprises in the Peoples' Republic of China, for example, the goal was production even if the product remained unsold. Estimates are needed of new market potential as well as reviews of current marketing procedures. What media are used in marketing? How effective are they and what are the distribution channels employed? What management information systems can or should be employed to promote new product development and to arrive at more accurate forecasts of sales and marketing costs?

5. Effectiveness of Management

The blame for SOE losses has frequently been laid at the door of management, not always justifiably. Government objectives and directives have often frustrated the best of managers. Presumably, a privatized company would not suffer from these impediments. Nevertheless, any buyer will want information on the quality of past management and the degree to which coherent policy planning has been used in allocating resources. To estimate this it will be necessary to examine:

- Methods that have been used in evaluating policy options, particularly in the financial area.

- External constraints on policy making.

- The effectiveness of strategic business planning and the quality and quantity of information available to managers for this purpose. What has been past capital investment policy and how informed have investment decisions been? How are priorities determined, alternative investments examined, and past experience appraised?

- Management's personnel policies and their effect on personnel attitudes. Has there been a history of unsatisfied grievances, strikes, and persistent disputes? What methods have been used to communicate with labor and involve unions in organizational management? What is the state of personnel records and what is management's assessment of personnel turnover? A detailed history of labor relations is an essential part of determining the attractiveness of a firm to the private sector. A firm that has suffered from chronic labor problems that have lowered productivity in the past will take time to recover until a new management is able to create confidence in its personnel practices. Transfer to private ownership will in most cases mean changes in personnel policies that may effect employee pension and benefit rights; these should be clarified prior to the sale.

While a close analysis of the internal financial problems and operating performance of the firm is a prerequisite to interesting a new buyer, equally important is an assessment of the environment in which the company does business. Legislation governing the operation of private firms should be reviewed. In what ways does it differ from that under which SOEs operate? Because of deep-seated distrust of the private sector in some LDCs in which the state has taken a primary role in development, the private sector may have restrictions applied to it that are not shared by SOEs. The regulatory framework imposed by the government may include price controls, labor limitations, profit restrictions, and foreign exchange access rules from which SOEs are exempted. Unless the government is prepared to relax some of these restrictions, buyer interest may be seriously diminished.

A detailed examination of the tax structure in which the privatized firm will be required to do business is also needed. Tax legislation applicable to privately owned companies, including income taxes, profit taxes, transaction taxes, and property taxes may not have been levied on SOEs. If the government is prepared to make either permanent or temporary concessions (possibly in the form of tax holidays) to private buyers of SOEs, the sale can be made substantially more attractive. In the case of privatized services, the buyer will want to be clear on the proposed extent of government regulation of rates, user fees, and limitations on return of capital invested before making a commitment. The key is equality of treatment; if competing SOEs are to remain, they must be subject to the same regulatory structure as private sector firms.

SELLING AN SOE

Once the detailed information on the firm has been assembled, the next step is to seek out possible buyers. If the government has chosen the route of divestment to a single buyer or an investor group, the question becomes one of locating potential purchasers. Normally neither the government nor donor agencies are equipped to deal with this; it requires highly skilled consultant services drawn from outside the country. The consultant should know in detail the market for the product being produced by the SOE (especially if it is designed for export), competitive market prices for the product, markets in the developed world, and possible new LDC outlets. Each product has its own market peculiarities, and there is no substitute for the detailed knowledge of a recognized specialist in the field. The specialist's advice on finding possible buyers will need to be followed closely.

The offer of the firm for sale must be made public, both domestically and internationally. A brochure can be written describing the firm, its background, and its present situation in general terms. The brochure should contain the sources and extent of more detailed available information, including that on conditions of sale. If the government has limitations on foreign ownership of the firm, these will have to be spelled out. It is important that the brochure contain sufficient detail so that potential purchasers can judge whether they are interested in pursuing the matter to the extent of making a formal bid. The amount of earnest-money deposit required for consideration of an eventual bid should be specified.

Apart from distribution of the brochure to internationally known firms in the same business, personal contacts by government officials, donor agency officers, investment bankers, and local entrepreneurs are additional ways of spreading the information. Advertisements in U.S. and European papers (as was done by the government of Panama in divestment of a hotel), indicating where the brochure may be obtained can also be used.

A number of options are available to accomplish the formal sale. The one chosen will depend on the individual circumstances of the firm, government preference, and judgment of the market for the specific product. Among these options is a negotiated sale to individuals or investor groups. Not all potential buyers will be acceptable to the government. Restrictions on foreign ownership may limit outside participation to a minority interest; if so, a joint local partner may have to be found. In such cases, the foreign joint partner may take over the management functions as well as providing capital and marketing skills (this was planned for some privatizations in Guinea, for example). The government may prefer to retain part ownership in a mixed arrangement. The official position on foreign investment should be fully clarified before the firm is offered for sale.

The identity of domestic buyers should be made public to avoid the accusation of sweetheart deals—i.e., that the firm is being sold at lower than market value to politically powerful local interests. Any indication that this may be the case will discourage interest in future privatizations. The position of the political leadership on bidding restrictions should be made explicit in the announcements.

In developed countries the most common technique of privatization has been a public share offering, as in the case of the largest British SOE divestments. If the capital market is sufficiently organized, there are several advantages to this method of sale in LDCs. It may accomplish the government's goal of redistribution of wealth; even more important, it will serve to introduce new segments of the population to the concept of share ownership. This has been one of the major attractions of privatizations in Jamaica and in the United Kingdom. Wide distribution of shares puts a premium on high quality of management of the firm, however, since, in the absence of government supervision, the operating responsibility now devolves into the managers' hands.

If the firm being divested is so large that it cannot be readily absorbed by the capital market, the government will have to market the offering in segments in order to avoid a "choking-off" effect—the drying up of capital resources for other development or industrialization. Timing of the offering is of critical importance. The SOE sale should not be initiated, for example, shortly after an offering of high-interest government bonds, which will have sopped up, at least temporarily, much of the available supply of capital.

The most difficult aspect of a share offering is determining the initial price of the shares when they are put on the market. The price can, of course, be set to reflect a market or asset-based price based on the valuation of the firm. This is the simplest option, but it does not take into account the advantages or disadvantages of setting the offering price above or below real market value. Professional advice from investment bankers may be needed to strike the best balance between a good return to the government and an attractive price to the potential buyer (particularly the small investor) so as to make the shares broadly available to the public. While a lower price may reduce the revenue obtained from the sale, it may be politically desirable as an illustration of the value of privatizing. Setting an initial offering price below market value also helps to assure that the offering will be widely taken up since there is the prospect of an immediate rise in share value, to the satisfaction of first time share owners. Too low a price may have the undesirable effect, however, of concentrating ownership in the hands of those who can afford to buy large blocks of shares, thereby defeating one of the possible purposes of the offering.

Limitations may have to be put on the number of shares that can be acquired by an individual or group and regulations made on the retention period for shares bought. Little is accomplished by enabling small investors to acquire shares if they are able to dispose of them at a profit to larger investors immediately after the sale. In the case of privatization of services in widespread public use, encouragement to buy can also be given by reducing user fees for new buyers. British Telecoms is an example; telephone subscribers' bills were reduced if shares were purchased. Payment for individual purchase of small numbers of shares on the installment plan can be an added inducement.

Pricing and sale of the offering is a matter requiring the highest technical skills and considerable experience that in most cases can only be obtained from brokerage firms or investment bankers. Before any firm is called in on consultation, its background and experience in stock offerings should be carefully checked, especially for similar work in LDCs; not all investment banking firms have experience in areas where markets are thin. Pricing the offering at lower than market rates, for example, is an advantageous technique for the government, but it has to be handled with considerable care. If the new shareholders lose on their investment, the whole privatization strategy may be undermined.

Giving away shares in an SOE being privatized is a somewhat unlikely option that may not find much support in LDCs but the government should be aware of it since it has certain unique political advantages. It creates an immediate and widespread public awareness of the positive results of privatization and improves the government's public image—it can be couched in terms of a return to the people of an investment they have already made from their taxes. It also eliminates some of the overhead costs associated with a public stock offering. But beyond these benefits, it has little to recommend it. It achieves no net revenue for the government; on the contrary, it reduces inflated "net worth" assets since the cost of the company must be immediately written off. The administrative costs of a give-away program are extremely high, and little public policy gain is made since with such diverse ownership, control of the company is effectively vested in the hands of its management. In the few instances where it has been tried, it has not been successful because the value of the shares declined rapidly after the give away so that the new owners received little of value from the privatization.

Various options for privatization to employee groups, labor/management buyouts, and employee stock ownership plans are discussed in chapter 2. They are mentioned here for the sake of completeness.

Valuation of Firms Being Privatized

Valuation of the industries or services that are candidates for privatization is one of the most necessary but at the same time most contentious aspects of privatization. The difficulty arises from the fact that there are normally at least two interested parties, the government as the current owner of the enterprise and the potential buyer and future owner. Each usually has a diametrically opposed objective—the government wants to realize as much from the asset as possible—at the very least, its past investment (and, it hopes, a profit); the buyer seeks to acquire the property as cheaply as possible. One of the pitfalls of a privatization program is that buyers tend to regard the voluntary privatization of a firm by a government as a forced divestment and will tend to base their offers on fire-sale rates.

Valuation becomes, then, not only a technical question of judging the real market value of the property concerned but also a matter of substantial political sensitivity. No government can afford to be exposed to the accusation that it is selling off the national goods cheaply to selected domestic entrepreneurs or to rapacious foreign investors (especially multinationals) who will seek to exploit the opportunity presented by divestment. Even if the property being sold has been losing money for a long period, with high, continuing subsidization needed to remain in business or has been badly mismanaged, the government will have to justify to its political opponents any decision to sell that involves writing down its investment, particularly if the sale offers the prospect of substantial employee redundancy.

In the final analysis, an acceptable valuation must arrive at a compromise between these two conflicting objectives. Only rarely will the government be persuaded that the sale price should correspond to the objective market value of the property, regardless of how the value figure has been arrived at. Ideally, the sale price should finally be suggested by an agency such as an investment bank, which is disinterested (and must publicly be seen to be) rather than by a group, however distanced from government, that could possibly be interpreted as gaining from the sale.

No satisfactory valuation of a firm to be privatized can be arrived at without close examination of factors extraneous to the immediate circumstances of the sale, such as the macroeconomic environment in which the firm has operated. The firm may have been unable to break even or make a profit because of government policies over which management had no control.

Social overhead objectives may have been imposed that are incompatible with profitable operation of the business. If so, an effort should be made to estimate their cost in order to give an accurate picture of the firm's potential if it were able to do business without such costs. The structure of government control over the firm may have played an important part in its operational inefficiencies and, therefore, its lack of profitability. Close official oversight may have prevented independent management decisions, or management may have been unable to determine precisely what the government's objectives for the firm were. SOEs that have been operated as closely as possible to a private business model have usually proved to be the easiest both to evaluate and to sell because management had been previously required to pay close attention to profitability.

Any valuation has to take into account the internal politics of the country concerned in an attempt to define clearly the government's stake in the firm being divested. If the firm being sold has figured strongly in the government's past policy pronouncements on industrialization or indigenization, it may be necessary to make special efforts to justify its being privatized to secure public acceptance of the sale. The government's overall objectives in privatizing are an indirect indication of the government's view of the worth of the firm and should be looked at carefully. If the government sees privatization primarily as a source of revenue, arriving at a lower sale price will be more difficult. If, on the other hand, the government views privatization of SOEs as a way of reducing expenditure or as a means of reducing its role in the economy to encourage growth of the private sector, the selling price may be somewhat more flexible.

The legal framework in which the firm to be divested has been initially created should be taken into consideration. The value of the firm may be diminished if it appears that lengthy and complicated actions by different arms of the government may be needed before the firm can be legally passed to new owners. This may become an important factor in the choice of firms to be privatized; firms whose ownership may be a matter of simple transfer by authority of a single ministry will be more readily saleable than those whose transfer requires court action. Attention must be paid to company law and the national commercial and regulatory codes. They may create complications in the sale that will effectively lower the value of the firm. The possibility of restriction of the business by government regulation must also be considered in those cases in which the firm is engaged in producing goods or services which are so-called natural monopolies, such as electric generating and distributing companies or transportation facilities. These may prove to be unsaleable regardless of their value because of fear that future regulation will restrict return on profits or withdrawal of capital investment.

Finally, the rather murky area of general forecasting of future world economic trends plays at least some role in valuation if the product is being produced for the foreign market. For domestic firms, the possibility of increased local consumption, if a higher quality product is envisaged by the buyer, may also figure in the calculation of value.

The technical financial analysis of an individual firm necessary to arrive at an estimate of its real worth should take into account the historical evolution of the firm from its establishment by the state to the present need for divestment. What prompted the government to create the firm—ideological conviction that state control was preferable, a need that was not being fulfilled in any other way, or a business opportunity from which profit could be made? In most cases, it may have been a combination of all three as well as other considerations. One further motive for establishing the firm may originally have been a desire to bring modern technology to the developing industrial sector. As the firm failed to prosper it may have been unable to keep up with technological advances in its product line and, consequently, lost any competitive advantage it may originally have had. The real value of the firm may to some degree also depend on whether the government sees the private sector as being able to replace the product produced by the SOE and, conversely, the potential buyers' estimate of whether the government really intends to relinquish control of production in the firm's field.

In all cases, estimates of future cash flow, based on studies of potential export markets, raw material sources, and the possibilities of seeking out previously unexplored markets, will be required. If the firm has been producing for the domestic market, can its local marketing and distribution networks be improved to a point at which greater profits can be created? SOEs have not been well known for their response to consumer preferences; indeed, some LDC firms have failed to reach profitability because consumers simply preferred to buy imported products of better quality or greater variety when they were available. Part of the valuation of the firm may rest on estimates of future possibilities inherent in new product lines, not on past production records. In any case, if the price structure for the product lines has been subject to government regulation, is the government prepared to allow market forces to set prices if the firm is privatized?

Valuation of the current financial state of the firm may be impeded by the absence of normally available business information. Any serious potential buyer will want financial information that meets international standards so as to be able to compare the company's performance with that of the industry as a whole. Full financial records are the exception rather than the rule for SOEs in developing countries. It may be necessary to reconstruct a financial history of the firm from such records as can be found, often a difficult, time-consuming, and expensive process that will not always produce satisfactory results. Important changes in assets, income, and costs over a given period may reveal hidden financial weaknesses, as will changes in liquidity and cash flow. Long- and short-term debt and possible hidden liabilities have to be identified. In addition, foreign investors will require precise information on official restrictions on repatriation of profits and capital. If it is likely that repatriation will be subject to a limited percentage annually (as in the case of investment derived from capitalization of debt in Chile), this will have to be factored into a buyer's estimate of the firm's value.

Apart from the purely financial aspect, an important part of valuing the firm rests on an estimate of the past and present capabilities of its management. A buyer will need to know how the managers have dealt with budgeting, planning, and personnel issues. How well trained are the managers in modern business practice? In many cases, managers of SOEs have in the past been seconded civil servants not necessarily attuned to the profit motive.

Increasing numbers of younger managers have had appropriate training, but they may not have been able to put it to the best use if they have had to answer to ministry representatives or a board composed of political appointees who have little knowledge of (or interest in) the business. Even well-trained managers cannot function effectively if they are continually being second-guessed by the board. If a potential buyer feels it necessary to replace the entire management structure, this may entail undue delay, if the current management has political influence, and prevent quick resumption of production, with resulting losses.

The government may feel that for political reasons full privatization may not be feasible regardless of its benefits. The government may decide to sell a controlling interest in the firm or to retain a majority share, in either case with the help of a private joint venture partner. The decision may be made to contract out overall policy direction and day-to-day operation of the firm to a management contractor. If the contractor takes an equity holding, an acceptable price for his holding will have to be agreed upon.

In some countries local privately owned companies have come into being which, because of more efficient management, have been able to compete successfully with SOEs without subsidization. A case in point is an iron foundry in Mogadiscio, Somalia, which the government was unwilling to divest completely. After a thorough business analysis, the consultant's recommendation was that the failing SOE be rescued by permitting a local privately owned and operated competing foundry to lease the property, making use of such working equipment as the state's firm possessed and integrating its production into that of the ongoing successful enterprise. It was also suggested that the range of products theoretically offered by the state foundry (many of which it could not, in fact, manufacture) be reduced to those that could be efficiently produced to meet local market demand.

Financing the Sale of an SOE

Many LDC governments feel that they must turn to donor agencies to finance the inevitable costs of privatization as well as for guidance and help in arranging the sale of large SOEs. Smaller privatizations in a few LDCs can be financed by local capital sources if an organized capital market exists. Private sector buyers may be able to pay the full cost from their own resources or with the help of local lending sources. A problem arises when the only groups with available capital may be unacceptable buyers for political reasons. If the government is chiefly concerned with divesting to local buyers, it may be prepared to grant easier or extended financial terms to them that would not be available to foreign purchasers.

Loans for the purchase of an SOE are unlikely to be easily available from local commercial banks. They are frequently more interested in short-term loans (preferably one year or less; at most three years) with greater security than a recently privatized SOE could provide. In most cases, rehabilitation of an SOE would require a longer period to produce a profit. Unless the local buyers of the divested firm have established a previous credit rating, commercial bankers, even if they are prepared to lend, may require full collateral or a government guarantee. Donor agencies do not customarily provide guarantees for commercial bank lending. In many LDCs commercial banks may find that their lending opportunities are restricted by government-imposed interest ceilings, making loans to the Treasury more profitable than those to private entrepreneurs.

Private or semiprivate intermediate financial institutions, such as development banks may be possible sources of loans. Such banks are able to make long-term loans, often with government or donor guarantees and on more reasonable terms. These loans are not always in the government's interest, however, if it is to be the guarantor. In case of default, the government may find itself the unwilling participant in a reverse privatization if it becomes necessary to repossess the divested firm.

International and bilateral donor agencies are increasingly becoming engaged in both technical and financial assistance to privatization. World Bank structural adjustment loans contain provisions for such assistance (as, for example, in the case of privatization of an oil refinery in Thailand). Conditions of the loans may require rehabilitation and ultimate privatization of subsidized SOEs or direct efforts to institute a privatization plan. The bank has been providing privatization assistance for almost a decade; some thirty countries have benefited from support for planning and strategy, for rehabilitation and restructuring of SOEs to prepare for privatization, and for studies on the effects of labor redundancy. With World Bank assistance, privatizations have taken place in Jamaica, Panama, Togo, and Niger, among other LDCs (Nellis and Kikeri, 1989:665–66).

In selected cases, the International Finance Corporation (IFC) may become a participating investor or a source of loans for a privatized firm. Its participation may encourage private sector investment or the mobilization of other financial sources. The IFC and the World Bank have embarked on a cooperative program to coordinate their responses to privatization requests. Assistance has also been provided to governments to make policy and regulatory changes to improve the environment in which the private sector operates. Using its LDC investment expertise, the IFC can provide both technical assistance in preparing for privatization and in the search for buyers.

Multilateral Development Banks (MDBs) are emerging as a potential source of financing privatization. They have expressed concern regarding expansion of the private sector in their member states but have hesitated to depart from their customary practice of lending to the private sector through governments or with government guarantee of the loans. The Asian Development Bank has begun lending directly to the private sector, but there has not yet been sufficient experience to judge the results.

New financial instruments have recently been utilized to encourage foreign investment in LDCs. Among the most important of these is the swapping of debts for equity. Debt capitalization is a relatively new concept in its application to developing countries, but it has gained momentum in a number of countries, particularly in Latin America. While its major application has hitherto been in the field of new investment, it has potential application to privatization in selected situations. The first formal announcement of a swapping program came from Chile in 1985, and similar programs have been initiated in Mexico, Argentina, Brazil, and the Philippines, among other states.

Debt-equity swapping is unlikely to become the panacea that will solve the international debt problem; nevertheless, there is growing incentive for countries to create value by repurchasing their debt at lower than face value. There is now a secondary market in the debt of certain countries; daily quotations are available and put and call options are being used.

In the swapping process, a foreign firm seeking to make an investment presents the proposal to the finance ministry of the country whose debt is sought for purchase, describing the project and the financing by debt capitalization. After coordination and review by the ministry and other parts of the government, the purchase of the debt is approved, with the percent of face value being clearly stipulated. The investing company then arranges to purchase debt at a deep discount. The total to be purchased equals the actual amount to be invested divided by the face value that the ministry has agreed to pay in local currency. The total of purchased debt is then canceled by the ministry by payment of local currency to the investing company. This currency is then used by the investor to purchase the capital stock of a newly organized or an existing company. This company then uses the local currency to make the desired investment (new plant, new equipment, or financial restructuring) by repayment of debt to local banks.

Swapping allows the finance ministry and the planning ministry to exert some control over new investment coming into the country in that the discount rate can be made more or less favorable depending on the type of investment being made or the location of facilities to be constructed or extended. Swapping can be used, then, by firms needing to make new investment or to recapitalize an existing subsidiary. In the latter case, swapping represents a reduction in local currency debt and an increase in equity. Attracting investment may require certain modifications of local tax laws; if the spread between purchase price of the debt and the local currency payout is treated as taxable gain, the investor may be less interested.

The possibilities for swapping depend, of course, on investment opportunities within the country. If there is little or nothing worth investing in or if the political climate is regarded as too risky, no amount of discounting of debt will attract new foreign investors. Not all debt is susceptible to swapping; depending on the conditions of the original syndicated loan agreement, specific limitations may apply. The sellers of debt being purchased are normally banks with relatively low exposure in the country concerned or those that have already written down the loans they hold (by increasing their loan reserves) to an amount below the face value of the loan—American regional banks are among this latter group.

Bringing together the three parties to the swap (the purchaser, the seller, and the government) is normally done by an intermediary, frequently an investment bank, which advises the government and prospective purchasers on the process, negotiates the investment project, and purchases the debt on behalf of the investor. In most cases, this requires several complicated steps and a knowledge of bureaucratic procedures and of the debt structure.

Apart from reduction of debt and debt servicing, swapping creates productive investment in the country which might not otherwise have been made, had not the opportunity existed to acquire local currency at a reduced rate. It helps also to develop local capital and securities markets if the government is prepared to require that all equity obtained by capitalization is listed on a local stock exchange.

Swapping may, in selected cases, have direct applicability to privatization. If a government is interested in privatizing an SOE and is prepared to seek a foreign joint partner, swapping may provide an inducement to a buyer who might not otherwise be interested. The price sought by the government for an enterprise may be unrealistically high if payment were required in hard currency, discouraging potential investors. If, however, payment can be made in local currency through a discounted swap, the price may become more attractive. Investment or commercial bankers can match buyers to swapping opportunities.

Donor agencies have recently begun to be involved in the swapping process. The World Bank, for example, is supporting the creation of legal and technical mechanisms in Zaire to permit swapping of external debt for equity in privatized SOEs, and in Togo banks are being strengthened to act as posting houses for swapping agreements. (Nellis and Kikeri, 1989:666).

The privatization of a steel foundry in Honduras provides an example of the use of a swap in completing the sale. The idle plant was sold to a group of U.S. investors after a number of other prospective buyers failed to express interest. The transaction was effected by means of a $2 million swap of debt of the Honduran National Investment Corporation. Of this, $1 million was for the firm's assets and the remainder was converted to local currency to be used by the investors as working capital. The innovative use of debt swapping in this case was perhaps the most attractive aspect of the deal in that both the government and the investors benefited. The investors exchanged debt for equity in a nonperforming asset that was expected subsequently to earn hard currency from its export sales. The government sold some of its hard currency debt; the investor paid a lower price for the local currency needed. This in turn reinforced the viability of the firm and compensated in part for the risk involved.

A second financial instrument applicable to privatization is the convertible bond that may be converted into shares of stock in a company at market rates. Even in those countries where capital markets have developed to a point at which there is an operating stock market, lack of sufficient offerings continues to discourage new investors. Investors still have an underlying suspicion that the small stockholder will be manipulated for the benefit of a few large families or groups that control the majority of the shares. Small investors tend to be more comfortable with the notion of a government guaranteed investment.

One way to bridge this gap is by the use of convertible bonds issued with a government guarantee. Buyers of these bonds may convert them into shares of stock that may rise in price, as will the bonds. So long as the buyers remain comfortable with the price of their shares, they can retain them for market trading. Should prices fall or become too volatile, they can dispose of the shares, relying on the government guarantee of the underlying bond. If the sale of SOEs can be financed by bond issues of this type, it may both encourage the small investor to come into the market as well as diversifying the offerings available for sale, including privatized firms.

MIXED OWNERSHIP AS A PROBLEM IN PRIVATIZATION

The proportion of the private-government mix of ownership may range from a substantial majority of the shares remaining in government hands to a token participation in which control is substantially vested in private shareholders. Mixed ownership dilutes the role of the private sector and frequently gives rise to doubts on the part of shareholders as to whether the enterprise will be operated on strictly commercial lines, so long as the interests of the government (which may be oriented to political or public policy ends) must be taken into account. Sometimes, however, if the government is unwilling or unable to accept full divestment, mixed ownership may have to be considered in developing a privatization program.

Although the government may be prepared to accept the idea of full divestiture, in some countries there may not be enough small shareholders capable of buying into the firm and no single indigenous buyer with sufficient resources to buy the enterprise outright. If one of the government's objectives in privatizing is to expand the capital market by increasing the numbers of small shareholders in the private sector (as is the case in Malaysia, for example), mixed ownership may be desirable for a temporary period while education of the public to the advantages of profits from shareholding continues. Some form of intermediary ownership (such as an intermediate financial institution or a development fund) may be desirable under these circumstances so that share purchase can be made as easy as possible.

Divestment of an SOE that involves continuing mixed ownership creates a number of policy considerations for donor agencies assisting in privatization efforts. A major question is whether such a divestment should be considered part of a privatization plan that qualifies for technical or other support. The decision on this point may involve an estimate of what the government's ultimate intentions for the SOE may be.

Even though committed to a divestment program, the government may insist on retaining some participation in an SOE because political considerations (accusations that the government is inappropriately selling off the national goods to private individuals, for example) may make it desirable to compromise on full divestment, at least temporarily.

Some SOEs may have popular symbolic value either because their products are well known and are thought highly of in the market or because national pride is involved in the existence of the firm (an example can be found in national oil companies such as Petro-Canada). The public would react strongly against complete loss of government control in such cases.

For public policy reasons, the government may wish to maintain some voice in decision making in the firm because the firm's products are perceived as vital to national security or because they concern exhaustible natural resources (such as minerals or petroleum). There may also be a long standing *dirigiste* tradition in the government (as, for example, in Mexico or Argentina) that makes the government disinclined to surrender full control to the private sector.

The asset may be too large to be privatized at once to a single buyer, domestic or foreign, even if the government is willing. It may be necessary to spin off viable parts of it in order to sell as large a share as the market will bear, particularly if the government's secondary objective is to increase popular acceptance of private sector activities.

It is not always easy to convince the government that, in sharing ownership with the private sector, its relationship to the former SOE has undergone a radical change. It may feel that it is required to demonstrate visibly that it has not abandoned the public interest. Even if it retains only a minority share, it may seek to exert pressure on the management to achieve public policy goals, some of which may not be compatible with the commercial objectives of a private sector firm.

The Impact of Mixed Ownership

Both the government and the private sector may derive advantages from mixed ownership. Positive cash flow results from the proceeds of the sale. The greater the share the government is prepared to surrender, the greater will be the proceeds. Moreover, a continuing cash flow from a well-managed, profitable company may be expected. The government may feel that a partially owned firm offers the opportunity to achieve public policy ends as well as profit. The private sector shareholders, on the other hand, may feel that the government will regard the firm with special favor because it has a continuing interest in it (although this perception is not conducive to free and open market competition).

But the disadvantages resulting from mixed ownership in the long run would appear to far outweigh its advantages. If the firm can achieve dynamic, profit-oriented private sector management, there will be decreasing opportunities for the government to use the corporation for its own public sector purposes. Should the government be prepared to commit itself at the time of sale to the divestment of its remaining share over a short period of time, investor confidence may be increased.

The prospect of mixed ownership may serve to reduce the amount the government realizes initially from the sale of the firm because the value of the shares (or of the firm as an entity) may be diminished. Financial markets will discount share prices because of the suspicion that the government will try to use the firm for its own ends. Even if the government claims that the firm will be expected to operate as a commercial enterprise after divestment, private shareholders may still discount prices, particularly if there is evidence that the government has previously used its powers to interfere in management decisions of SOEs.

The government must give convincing assurances that it does not intend to interfere in the day-to-day operation of the firm by removing its representatives from direct contact with the management and by publicly announcing a detailed plan for gradual withdrawal as a shareholder over a reasonable period of time. Any departure from these arrangements will cause a sharp fall in share prices, to the disadvantage of the public and private owners.

Even with partial government ownership, there are definite limits to the government's ability to use its shares to force the firm to serve public policy interests if the firm is operating in a competitive environment. Any action by the government that would seriously damage the interests of private shareholders would reduce the firm's profitability. Privatization assumes that market forces, not public policy, will be the operative norm.

The normal commitment of managers in private firms is to work in the commercial interests of the shareholders. Any reduction in the government's control of a corporation through privatization creates a corresponding rise in the autonomy of the managers and hence in their ability to resist the government's demands. Even a minority of private shareholders can exert considerable political influence as a pressure group, especially if they happen to be wealthy or prominent in the community. Thus, the government's position as a shareholder is weakened because it becomes subject to the forces of public opinion. Mixed ownership may, in fact, put an even larger degree of decision-making power in the hands of management than would be the case with full private ownership. The number of private shareholders may not be large enough to effect management changes and, if the government tries to do so, it exposes itself to charges of interference.

Separating Commercial and Policy Objectives

Other devices exist for separating the commercial objectives of firms to be privatized while preserving the policy objectives of the government. The firm to be privatized may be split by selling it not as an integrated unit but as two or more firms, one of which would be designated to carry out policy objectives that are clearly not commercially viable. The commercial activities can be divested as a separate company entirely divorced from government participation and subjected to the full force of the market. In this firm the government takes the same risk as the private investor, and no effort should be made to rescue the firm in case of failure. A distinct, wholly state-owned company can be created that has a continuing policy role but no requirement for profitability.

Such splitting might be considered, for example, in the case of a capital intensive mining operation that would be unattractive to the private sector. The cost of exploration and extraction would be borne by the government firm, and the processing and marketing of the mineral handled by the commercial arm. In another case, high risk exploration for petroleum resources could be separated from the commercial refining operations and the wholesale or retail distribution of the product. Crude oil would be acquired from the government company or other sources at prevailing market prices. There is no reason, of course, why the policy-oriented company could not have private sector participation, if investors could be found. It may be desirable to establish the policy-oriented firm as a holding company for the government shares in the commercial firm; this would, however, require commitment on the part of the holding company management not to interfere with commercial management decisions.

In order to make even clearer the divorce between policy and commercial interests, a collective arm's-length holding company for the shares of all privatized firms in which the government retains some participation can be created. This company's function would be to monitor the performance of the firms in which the government has an interest and to report back to the responsible government officials. It could also be made responsible for conducting the negotiations for the sale of firms being privatized; this, however, may leave the relationship too close between the firms and the politicians.

Protecting the Government's Interest in a Partial Privatization

The government may be reluctant to initiate privatization because of the fear that it will lose control over crucial aspects of national industrial development. It is possible to overcome this fear by demonstrating that the government's interests can be protected after divestment by a variety of devices, even if it remains only a minority participant. Although privatization means exposing the corporation to market forces, the success of any mixed ownership corporation depends on the way in which the government's interest in the firm is organized. The government's relationship to the other shareholders becomes of critical importance—to an even greater degree if the government retains a majority holding. The problem becomes one of keeping the private shareholders and other potential investors convinced that market factors control the firm's operations, while at the same time satisfying bureaucratic demands for accountability to the responsible ministries.

It may be possible to persuade the government that its regulatory powers can be substituted for ownership, thus making full privatization acceptable. The government will be in a position to collect tax revenues from a profitable service company, while regulating charges for its services to the public.

The government may eventually be persuaded that its representatives do not need to sit on the board of the firm in order to ensure that the public interest is served. Indirect representation may well be to the advantage of both parties; by maintaining its distance, the government may improve the firm's competitive position.

There are firms whose chief customers have been, and will continue to be after privatization, the government itself. Firms making munitions, for example, come under this category. The fact that there is an assured market for the firm's production may be of some comfort to the private shareholders. On the other hand, the government may be able to apply pressure on the firm by threatening to remove its main supply contract if alternative sources of supply exist. This may ensure that the privatized firm will produce according to government specifications and requirements, but it may also mean that it will have to accept lower profit margins.

The government may have recourse to a "golden share" provision, either to protect what it views as a vital policy interest or, in the case of more developed economies, to forestall a takeover of the privatized firm by a competing firm. The golden share is a very convenient device whereby the government is provided in the sale agreement with special voting rights (in effect, a veto) over some majority decisions by the board or the stockholders. If the golden share is used, the number of shares held by the government becomes irrelevant; it may be exercised by a single share if necessary. The golden share has a chilling effect on potential buyers, however, unless its use is clearly restricted prior to the sale (by legislation or preferably by contract that, if breached, can be enforced by the courts) to very specific and highly limited situations. If the government is empowered to use its golden share powers too often or too easily, the whole point of the privatization could be vitiated. The golden share arrangement may prove particularly useful in LDCs in which the government is exposed to political attack for selling the national goods. It permits effective privatization while making the government's vote available at critical points, so that it cannot be argued that the government has ever lost control. Some major privatizations in Great Britain have included this feature.

It is also possible for the government to retain its policy objectives, while leaving a privatized firm to operate freely under commercial conditions, by the use of a general public policy instrument applying to an entire sector of industry. Incentive packages for petroleum or mineral exploration can be handled in this way, for example, as can provisions for maintaining national or even restricted ethnic ownership (as in the case of Malaysia). Using a generalized sectoral instrument is nondiscriminatory and, therefore, avoids the accusation that a mixed ownership firm is receiving special favors or must operate under special limitations. A focused instrument, which is a variant on the general instrument, can be applied to a regional development objective to promote industrial concentration in a localized area.

The government can always preserve the ultimate right to require a mixed ownership firm to undertake activities that would clearly not be in its best commercial interests. Requiring the firm to hire excess numbers of employees during periods of high unemployment or regulating prices or production levels for public policy reasons are examples. In such cases, the government should use a directed compensation instrument to compensate the firm for the additional costs incurred. The question of measuring such costs is not always easy, however, and it may lead to prolonged negotiations between the management and the government, especially if indirect or overhead costs are involved over a period of time.

Too many demands of this nature will eventually reduce the effectiveness of the management and weaken the firm by leading to an erosion of investor confidence. Such intrusions into the commercial activities of the firm may not, in any case, be the most cost effective way of attaining the government's objective.

Whatever mechanism is used to protect the government's interests, machinery for performance evaluation and accountability to the appropriate level of government should be in place before a partial sale is completed. If the government insists on mixed ownership, it should be encouraged to examine its reasons closely; it may discover that no real public policy objective is being served by mixed ownership. If this is found to be true, the firm should be sold entirely to the private sector.

If mixed ownership is unavoidable, either for overriding political, security, or other reasons or is seen by the government as a transitional step, the major objective should be to divorce commercial operation of the mixed firm from public policy objectives and to make the fact of this divorce as clear as possible to the public and especially to the shareholders. It is desirable that the government become at most a minority shareholder at the outset or if not, that a plan to reduce, over a specified time period, its holding to a minority share be announced at the time of the sale. Even if provision is made for special voting rights, private shareholders will be reassured if the government's objectives are made clear. Demonstration that the government intends to maintain an arm's-length relationship to all privatized firms in which it retains an interest by creating a separate mechanism in which the government's holdings will be held will serve to buoy the market price of shares over a period of time.

MANAGEMENT CONTRACTING AS A PRELUDE TO PRIVATIZATION

Management contracting as a means of rescuing SOEs that are chronic money losers has come into increasing favor in the developing world as pressures to reduce subsidy costs rise and greater efficiency is demanded of the enterprises. In its simplest form, a management contract is an agreement by a firm to provide management control and operating functions of a company in return for a fee. The goal of a management contract is to produce cost-effective and profitable operation. If the government is committed to a privatization program, the ultimate goal of a management contract may be to make the firm attractive to potential private sector buyers, either domestic or, in joint enterprise form, foreign investors. In any case, management contracting—putting management in private hands is a first step in the process of transferring ownership to the private sector. A long-term leasing arrangement may accomplish the same ends, particularly if political considerations make outright sale undesirable or economic conditions would force sale at a bargain price.

Management contracts may take a wide variety of forms; in fact one of their great attractions is that they are almost infinitely flexible. They may contain virtually any terms on which both parties agree. But a management contract must be clearly distinguished from a situation in which an outside executive is brought in for a temporary period to assume management direction as an employee of the firm. Management contracts universally have three elements—the owner, the managing firm, and the personnel who are assigned as employees of that firm to carry out the responsibilities required under the contract. The contracting firm usually requires full guarantee of operational autonomy and decision making with complete freedom from interference by government ministries during the term of the contract. This autonomy normally includes control over wage rates and hiring and firing—powers which the government as owner is often reluctant to concede. It is important to distinguish between a management *consulting* contract (under which management advice is given, but need not necessarily be taken) and a contract in which full management authority is granted for the duration of the agreement.

For the owner (i.e., the government), a management contract provides independent direction of the firm, as well as transfer of modern management technology and knowledge of production methods. At the same time the government retains ownership of the firm as a counter to political charges of selling state-owned facilities to private owners. A management contract may, where a foreign contractor is employed, provide access for the firm to new external markets and international capital sources.

For the managing contractor, a contract provides compensation for services throughout the term of the contract, in some cases with no equity risk involved. Additional compensation through procurement or product marketing arrangements may be written into the contract. It may also provide experience for the contractor's employees in managing under difficult operating conditions.

But there are disadvantages for both sides in a management contract. The owner loses effective operating control over the firm and the ability to use board and management positions for political purposes, as well as having to pay the cost of contract fees. Disadvantages for the contractor include the risk that the government may renege on the agreed fees. The legal costs and the time involved in enforcing payment may not be cost effective even if a unilateral termination clause in case of failure by the government to pay agreed costs is written into the contract. The possibility exists, moreover, that the government may be unable to resist the temptation to improperly interfere in operational decisions.

Structuring a Management Contract

It is imperative that the government and the manager be clear at the outset on the objectives of the contract and that these objectives be spelled out in detail in the contract language. There must also be a clear division of responsibility between the parties with delineation of the precise role (if any) the government's representative on the board is expected to play. Both parties will need "escape clauses.'' In the case of the government, the right to intervene, for example, may be desirable in the case of mass political discontent if the industry is a producer of necessities, such as bread or beer.

The question of equity participation by the management contractor is a matter of negotiation. Some contractors (especially U.S. firms) will not undertake a contract without equity in the firm, arguing that without this, there is less incentive to provide profitable management. If the government retains majority control, the management contractor will normally insist on full operational control to protect its equity. In the case of hotel leasing and in franchise and lease-back arrangements, the contractor may undertake management alone, either in return for a fixed fee or fee plus a share of the profits. Both public and private sector firms under management contract have to work within the overall context of the government's macroeconomic policy. Prospective managers may insist that certain changes in commercial and labor codes be made before they will consider undertaking a contract.

For management contracting to be effective in rehabilitating a failing SOE, the firm's problems must derive from an evident lack of certain skills or capabilities in current management which, if brought in by the contractor, would provide some prospect of improving the firm's profitability. It is always possible that the firm cannot be rescued by any management change and should either be sold outright if a buyer can be found or liquidated.

The government, as owner, must have a realistic expectation of what a management contract can accomplish. If the chief concern is with immediate returns in the form of profits at the expense of building a solid base for expansion of the business, the government is likely to be disappointed. Management contractors do not perform miracles; a firm in need of such services is probably going to require a long turn-around time, not only to achieve internal efficiency but to create better markets for its product.

Management contracting has often been regarded as applicable chiefly to the industrial sector. However, some of the most successful contracts have dealt with agriculture—an example is the Kenana sugar plantation in Sudan, where 125,000 acres have for some years been under the management of an American firm. Apart from the growing and marketing of the plantation's main product, the firm has branched out into production of electricity from sugar biomass, which supplies the needs of the operation and feeds surplus power into the national grid. Modern large-scale agrobusiness is capital-intensive and requires management, technical, and marketing capabilities that make it peculiarly adaptable to contracting.

Service industries such as transportation (particularly at the municipal level), airlines, hotels, port facilities, and, less frequently, railroads, have been the subject of contracts. Since these state-owned facilities often do not provide opportunity for the manager to take equity, the contracts are somewhat simpler to draw up. This applies equally to contracting for public utility management.

Paying the Management Contractor

In any discussion of the financial arrangements of the contract, it is important to remember that the government is paying for services for which there may not be a predetermined market value. The owner needs the skills, experience, and contacts the manager's personnel can provide; depending on the specialized nature of the firm's product, the choice of potential contractors may be very restricted and hence the fees will be high. For political reasons the government will seek to keep the cost as low as possible. The negotiations will be affected by the government's perceived need to rehabilitate the firm and by the manager's calculations of the indirect benefits that may be derived in business experience, separate material supply contracts, and marketing arrangements.

Two types of financial agreements under which contracts have been undertaken are the annual fixed fee without equity participation and the fixed fee with incentive. The annual fixed fee without equity is one of the more attractive arrangements from the point of view of the managing company but much less attractive from the government's point of view. The manager receives a guaranteed fixed sum (which usually includes an inflation protection clause) in addition to any other indirect benefits. From the government's viewpoint, this may represent an unacceptably high figure if political opposition arguments must be met; it may be difficult to find comparative figures to determine whether the proposed fee is fair. Moreover, the fixed fee arrangement lacks the critical factor of guaranteed performance. Without equity incentive, the contractor has no reason except professional reputation to get results; the fee will be collected in any case. It is not surprising, then, that this arrangement is relatively rare. However, in countries where the risk of political upheaval and consequent harm to the manager's personnel or damage to the managing firm's reputation is perceived to be high, the government may find no alternative.

A reimbursable fee-plus incentive arrangement may be made, but this has the disadvantage, from the government's point of view, of uncertainty as to the ultimate cost of the contract. A combination of payments may include the base fee plus an incentive addition, fees based on production, or a percentage fee on gross revenue with a minimum floor. The manager normally seeks an incentive related to sales (preferably calculated on a quarterly basis) while the owner finds one linked to profits more advantageous. If special services beyond purely management are desired, the contractor may insist on separate payments; it is preferable, however, that these be built into the general payment, or at least limited by a total expenditure figure.

If no equity in the firm is taken, the manager's risk is reduced; on the other hand, the chances of substantial profit will be forgone if the enterprise can be made highly successful. Ultimately, the management company can take only a limited degree of commercial risk, and the government can only make limited tax or foreign exchange concessions as levers to bargain for a reduction in management fees. Some contracting firms argue that the cost of their fees for a long-term contract may well be less than the cumulative cost to the government of the subsidies that would be required to keep an inefficient firm in business.

U.S. firms have an additional incentive to engage in long-term contracts because of domestic tax breaks available to them for work outside the country. If these can be combined with additional tax incentives offered by the owner, or the prospect of substantial profit sharing, U.S. contractors will be inclined to assume greater risks in the the type or condition of the firm they are prepared to manage. In the final analysis, the cost of the contract and the form of payment will represent a trade-off between all of these conflicting interests.

On balance, contracting has proved to be a promising solution if effective management can turn around a failing enterprise or provide production and marketing avenues in capital-intensive heavy industries, such as mining or petroleum production, in which LDCs lack technical skills. Not every failing SOE's problems can be cured by improving the management, but as a technique leading to private sector interest in acquisition of a state owned enterprise, it deserves serious consideration.

4

The Privatization of Services

Attention to privatization in the developing countries has initially been focused primarily on the divestment and sale of state-owned industrial enterprises, in part because it was in this sector that heavy losses were causing the most serious drain on national treasuries. But privatization is now being increasingly considered in two other sectors of LDC economies, services and agriculture.

The service sector has attracted government interest because of the competition that has arisen between the services provided by the government and those of higher quality now being provided by the private sector, often at lower cost. The services the private sector is capable of supplying range from municipal refuse collection, street cleaning, and bus transportation to generation of electricity for the national grid and telecommunications networks. Privately supplied services in public health and in education are beginning to play more important roles.

PRIVATIZING MUNICIPAL SERVICES

Municipal services are particularly well adapted to privatization. In the case of urban transportation, government services have operated at substantial losses while competing privately run buses have begun to provide better service on a cost-efficient basis. As a result, city governments have become interested in turning over to private firms a service that has long required heavy subsidization. In Bangkok, for example, the municipal administration has for some time been seeking a buyer for its bus services. Service has already been successfully privatized in Calcutta and privatization is under discussion in Amman and Dakar.

Divestment of municipal transport faces a major political hurdle, however, in that the private transporter is almost certain to increase user fees. Although there is evidence that consumers are willing to pay for reliable and frequent service, nevertheless, there is a limit to their ability to accept increased fares charged by private operators if they rise too steeply. In consequence, private buyers are likely to face regulation of their profit margin, which discourages investment in new equipment and route extension. A balance must be struck between the consumers' willingness to pay for better service and the perception that they are being exploited by the private sector operator. It is possible for the government to retain ownership of the system while offering it to the private sector on a competitive leasing or franchise arrangement. By so doing, the government is relieved of maintenance costs and capital investment in new equipment. The franchise should be open to competitive bidding; otherwise, there is a danger of exchanging an inefficient official monopoly for an equally inefficent private monopoly.

Other municipal services, such as trash collection, road and park maintenance, and even municipal parking can be treated similarly. The Malaysian capital, Kualalumpur, has contracted out these services for some time. In Nairobi, the City Commission has sought donor assistance to develop a plan for privatization of solid waste disposal. Contracts for refuse collection and disposal for all but the city center would be given to separate firms for various sections of the city to create competition among contractors for the highest levels of service. A similar system has been developed for Santo Domingo, the capital of the Dominican Republic. In Abidjan, Cote d'Ivoire, the municipal water supply system has for some time been in private hands, based on the model of French cities. The distribution infrastructure of water is usually provided by the government, while operation is carried out by the private firm. In some service franchise operations, the government receives a fixed fee; in others a profit-sharing arrangement can be negotiated. In the case of essential services such as water, the government may regulate the price charged to customers, while allowing for reasonable profit after maintenance charges are paid.

Municipal services are particularly suited to this type of franchising arrangement because entry costs are fairly low. Unlike the purchase of a goods-producing firm, a heavy initial investment is not required, and capital replacement costs can be spread over a longer period. There is also the incentive of a reasonably secure market for the service provided. But the government must be prepared to deal with strenuous objection to privatizing from the municipal employee trade unions who expect job losses.

Several countries have tried experiments in contracting for road maintenance with varying success. When budgets are tight, road maintenance is often considered among the expenditures with the lowest priority. To cut the cost of maintaining large amounts of equipment scattered throughout a wide area, to meet the local political demand for frequent maintenance, and to achieve greater flexibility, national or regional governments have contracted out maintenance to the private sector. In Kenya, small local contractors have developed capacities to undertake full maintenance contracts. In Zaire, the Office des Routes contracted, with donor encouragement, for mechanical and manual maintenance and rehabilitation of over five hundred kilometers of roads. Similar experiments have been tried in Madagascar. Success depends on the capabilities and skills that small contractors can muster; performance is subject to criticism by the local community, which leads to a uniformly higher level of work.

PRIVATIZING ENERGY SUPPLIES

One impediment to the more rapid spread of service privatization has been the popular perception of "entitlement"—i.e., what services do the populace traditionally expect government to supply without user cost? In some countries, user expectation is unexpectedly high; in Kingston, Jamaica, for example, user charge measured by meter for electricity supplied to dwellings is deeply resented and extraordinary efforts are made to evade these charges by bypassing meters. The result is that there is little likelihood that a private buyer can be found at present for the electric plant.

Elsewhere in the world, however, privatization of energy is being actively pursued. In Southeast Asia several firms are producing energy for their own needs from refuse from their main operations (such as bagasse from sugar cane). Energy that is surplus to requirements is fed into local or national distribution grids, and payment is received from the government. Divestment to the private sector of power-generating firms has not been widespread, however, in part because the high capital cost both of production and distribution networks makes them unattractive to investors.

Many governments are concerned with making electricity available as widely as possible to rural consumers as well as to the urban population. But the cost of providing service to isolated rural communities is often so high that private firms are discouraged from undertaking it. One way to compensate for this is to have the government fund expansion of the grid to meet rural consumer demand and the private sector generate the electricity and maintain the system. In some cases, it may be more feasible to encourage creation of privately owned local networks serving limited areas rather than expanding the national grid over long distances to small numbers of users. Imposing a higher user fee on rural areas or requiring new customers to pay connection costs is politically difficult.

Energy systems traditionally have been owned and operated by the state. Because they have not been profitable, they often lack modern technology and are seriously undercapitalized. As a result they are of little interest to investors, domestic or foreign, who would prefer to concentrate on new plant construction free of the burden of previous debt, labor restrictions, and aging equipment.

More LDCs are being forced to liquidate outmoded generating facilities and are now turning to the new concept of build, own, operate, transfer (BOOT) for construction of new plants. Under this plan the investors (foreign, local, or a consortium of both) find the financing and build and operate the new facility for a fixed length of time. At the end of the the that time, ownership is transferred to the government or to a group of local private investors. In theory, the initial investors recover their capital outlay and a reasonable return over the agreed period (twenty years or more) but it is possible to delay recovery of part of the investment until the point of transfer.

From the LDC government's viewpoint, BOOT has a number of advantages, particularly in capital intensive, high technology ventures, such as electric utilities or communications facilities. It can also be used in high cost construction of toll roads and bridges. In most LDCs, governments and the private sector could not find the necessary financing under current conditions for such a large investment. But under BOOT, development plans can proceed that will enable smaller industries to grow up using the newly available power resources. Private sector initiative can be used in an industrial sector hitherto the exclusive preserve of government, and the project can be assured of the most modern available technology. Domestic partners are given the opportunity to gain experience through working with large international firms. While the final transfer may be to the government, capital market development over the twenty-year operating period may make possible transfer to the local private sector. An example of BOOT has been undertaken in Turkey, with construction of an electricity generating plant financed by American and European sources and the help of a World Bank loan.

BOOT projects are not without risk, but it a risk that is shared by all parties. Foreign investors are subject to the risk of nationalization by a succeeding regime, but no government could attempt this without irreparably damaging its world credit rating. The government may offer tax and other incentives for the project at a cost to the Treasury, but these are far outweighed by the advantages inherent in a BOOT initiative.

PRIVATIZING TELECOMMUNICATIONS SYSTEMS

Telecommunications is becoming one of the more active candidates in the field of privatization of services. With expansion of the private sector in the LDCs, a growing need arises for rapid and reliable communications, not only overseas but in-country as well. Many LDCs suffer from technologically primitive internal communications systems inherited from the former colonial administrations. These have only sporadically and locally been updated, often with inadequate or incompatible equipment. In many cases it is virtually impossible to communicate by telephone with areas outside the main centers, and even communication within the major cities is slow and frustrating. Larger foreign companies have installed their own radio communications, but local businesses have increasingly chafed under the inadequate telephone systems. In such cases privatization is often being driven more by the forces of technological change than by government intention.

As a result of local pressures, many governments have found themselves faced with the dilemma of replacing antiquated systems with modern equipment at a capital cost beyond their reach or finding the business community deserting the national telephone network to establish its own network by private radio or satellite systems. The alternative is to allow the private sector to take over the functions now poorly carried out by a government department. The successful privatization of British Telecommunications and the Japanese system over the past three years have provided examples for at least one country, Malaysia, to begin the process of allowing a private company to assume the responsibility for the internal telephone system. Other countries are following suit. In Hong Kong, the eastern Caribbean, and Sri Lanka, a private British company, Cable and Wireless, has either assumed control or is in process of buying a majority share in internal and external communications. In 1988, Jamaica privatized its telecommunications services.

Surrendering control of the telephone network is not easy for any government, however. Security considerations play an important role; the armed forces are very reluctant to see communications in private hands and are likely to resist any move in this direction. Most governments are faced with the often politically and bureaucratically sensitive problem of transforming the traditional ministry of posts and telegraphs into a private company—a process that may be long and difficult. An alternative to outright sale of the entire service is to spin off individual functions. In Malaysia, building and maintenance of lines and substations had been privately contracted even under the ministry.

To ensure expansion of the network into rural areas, the government may, as in the case of electricity, have to pay the costs as a form of subsidy. This was planned in the case of the sale of telecommunications in Grenada. Since privatization of services in these fields is both complex and lengthy, it is likely that any government embarking on it will need substantial technical advice. In Malaysia, the same British brokerage firm that handled the sale of British Telecommunications was hired as an advisor.

PRIVATIZING HEALTH AND EDUCATION SERVICES

Since 1980 experiments in privatizing parts of the educational system have taken place in a few LDCs. They have followed two main lines, the private funding of educational services and institutions and private sector control of some schools, often of an elite nature. In Kenya, unaided Harambee schools have existed for some years, and in 1988 they constituted 90 percent of private secondary school enrollment. Local communities contribute the labor, cash, and building materials to build schools more cheaply than can the government. Teachers are supplied by the government. Their scholastic level appears to be on a par with government-operated secondary schools.

In Chile, the government has subsidized a growing number of tuition-free schools operated by the private sector. With the blessing of the government, these have increased some 65 percent since 1984. The tradition of private education has long been established in the Philippines, including universities and various types of secondary schools.

Many of the examples of privatizing education in LDCs reflect a higher demand at all levels than can be absorbed by the officially operated school system. To meet the increasing demand for universal primary and secondary education, many governments have no alternative than to turn to the private sector, whether in the form of privately operated schools or those established by cooperative community action. Where private schools have greater resources, they may be able to provide more varied curricula and a higher standard of teaching than can government schools. These new standards and educational innovations may spill over gradually into the public schools.

The privatization of health services in the developing world is also a response to greater popular demand, not only for wider availability of health care but also for higher quality of the care provided. Assistance in this field may be expected to become a major factor in donor programming in the coming years. The U.S. Agency for International Development, for example, has concentrated its work in four fields:

1. Local Production of Commodities and Equipment. Local firms have been assisted in Central America and Africa to produce oral rehydration salts for widespread distribution, and some help has been given to local production of vaccines.

2. Employer Provided Services. Help has been directed to establishing employer-supported services in family planning and child survival. As employment increases, the number of firms able to offer such services will rise; some companies are already extending their employee services to surrounding communities.

3. Privatizing Health Facilities. The transfer of ownership and operation of health care facilities from the government to the private sector is only now beginning in LDCs. Entire units, such as hospitals, may remain in government hands, but management may be contracted out, or hospital services, such as laundry and feeding, may be spun off into private sector contracts, as has been the case in American Samoa. Special attention has been devoted to assisting microenterprises in the health field (those with ten or fewer employees), such as nurse-midwife associations in Ghana, to improve their services. This trend will develop more rapidly as governments become convinced that the private sector can deliver services more cheaply and greater numbers of privately run medical centers are created.

4. Privately Operated Health Insurance Services. Donor help is being requested from LDCs for studies in the establishment of private health insurance plans and health maintenance organizations, as well as expansion of the capabilities of private insurance firms to provide prepaid health coverage. This aspect of the privatization of health care is only now beginning to emerge in the developing world as a matter of public concern. So far it has been hampered by rising costs of such plans as a result of inflation.

The populations of developing countries have expected government provision of such social services as exist, but it is becoming evident that financial and personnel limitations will prevent sufficiently rapid expansion of service levels to meet the demands of a growing and better educated citizenry. There is evidence that even the poorer elements of the population are prepared to pay user fees for high quality and convenience of education and health services. Under these circumstances, the only alternative for the government is to turn to the private sector, particularly in professional fields where salaries can outrun those paid by the civil service. In many countries the private sector is not yet organized or equipped to provide all the services needed. In the more remote and, therefore, less profitable rural areas, government agencies will continue to be needed. In the more highly concentrated urban and peri-urban areas, however, private sector providers will gradually replace government agencies with better, if not necessarily cheaper, service networks.

5

Privatization and the Agricultural Sector

RETURNING AGRICULTURE TO THE PRIVATE SECTOR

The agricultural sector has been the subject of state intervention in most LDCs at least since the colonial period. Marketing services have frequently been government monopolies as have input services, pricing, and overall management of production. Almost universally, state intervention has proved to be a disaster, in terms of food supply as well as from the viewpoint of the peasant farmer.

Parastatals in the form of marketing boards have been the major instrument of state control and direction of the agricultural sector. The use of marketing boards derives in part from the experience of the colonial period in which they were instituted to maintain export supplies. After independence the system was continued because the new leadership was faced with the political problem of providing supplies of food grains at cheap prices to satisfy the demands of the politically vocal urban population. The peasant producers were expendable because they lacked a unified voice to become a political force. Agriculture was the predominant economic activity in most LDCs, and it therefore was expected to provide the most accessible source of capital for the new industrial base dreamed of by the nationalist leaders. Without this source of capital, the leaders claimed, there would be no increase in urban employment nor could an import substitution program be created that would free the newly independent country of the economic shackles of colonialism. The marketing boards were designed to maintain the sources of foreign exchange through controlled agricultural exports and to furnish the means of promoting the modernization of the economy. The farmers were consistently the losers from the outset in this new vision, although ultimately the state was an even greater loser since the system provided little or no incentive to the producer to increase the agricultural surplus for the export market.

Governments justified the marketing boards as instruments to protect the peasant farmer from exploitation by private traders. But the monopoly exercised by the officially designated agencies more often than not proved more exploitive than market forces while at the same time becoming a wasteful and inefficient use of scarce public resources. By its very nature, the buying and selling of agricultural products in a small-holder situation requires decentralized activity over large areas, involving close interpersonal relations. Local traders knew their customers, could be flexible in their transactions, and could respond quickly to changing market conditions. They may have profited at the expense of the farmers but often less so than did the government agents.

Apart from the inevitable inefficiencies of a bureaucracy that sought to centralize control of a process that did not lend itself to close supervision, the marketing boards required costly storage facilities and a large and highly trained staff, whose skills and energies might have been better employed in more technical development projects. The boards provided sinecures for the politically unemployed, offered large-scale opportunities for corruption, and failed to provide the input services that might have helped to create greater production. The price distortions resulting from conflicting government objectives only added to the deteriorating agricultural situation for which the boards were in large part responsible.

Both bilateral and international donors frequently served to exacerbate the problem. Food grains were provided on concessional terms to meet the governments' requirement to provide adequate food supplies at reasonable cost to the urban populations. As a result, the need for fundamental changes in agricultural policy was masked and the governments could afford to ignore the increasingly critical shortages in domestic production. Technical assistance to agriculture was provided through government agencies on a project basis that, though beneficial to the immediate recipients, failed to take into account the political environment in which agricultural policy was developed.

In many developing countries, ideological considerations played an important part in the government's view of the role of agriculture after independence. Those leaders who espoused socialism as a model for development placed emphasis on collectivization at the expense of the traditional individual farmer, particularly in Africa. The result was the creation of state farms or collective farming experiments of the type espoused by Julius Nyerere in Tanzania, Kenneth Kaunda in Zambia, or Sékou Toure in Guinea. Invariably, where the African farmer no longer benefited from the results of increased individual effort, production declined, marketing facilities failed, and care of the land was neglected.

Two decades of policy mistakes and ineffective administration by the marketing boards, as well as factors beyond the control of the governments (such as drought and changes in world commodity prices), brought decline in agricultural production in many LDCs, especially in Africa, to a point at which countries that had formerly been self-sufficient became heavy net importers of food. It should be added, however, that, because of controlled prices, the marketing board managers were not always at fault for the failure to produce satisfactory results. Reluctant governments were finally forced by circumstances and by donor pressure to consider radical changes in their approaches to agricultural policy. One of the foremost of these was privatization.

Compared with privatization of industries, however, the problems in agriculture have been much more complex and, in some ways, more deep-seated. It was not simply a question of eliminating the marketing boards and turning over their functions to a waiting private sector. In a few countries, such as Turkey, India, and Mexico, which could afford subsidization, the government was able to use the boards to provide new technologies that increased production.

In many cases, fundamental government attitudes toward agriculture had to be changed. So long as the policy was designed to favor vested interests in official circles or certain limited groups in the population, such as the urban minority, no liberalization allowing for entry by the private sector would succeed in increasing production. Macroeconomic policies, such as foreign exchange restrictions, overvalued currencies, and import restrictions were often as much of a hindrance to agricultural progress as were the marketing boards. Government taxation of agriculture to provide resources for industrialization had reached a saturation point. Farmers were forced to pay beyond their capacity and, in the time-honored rural reaction, they either limited production to their own needs or clandestinely moved any surplus out of reach of the marketing agency. But where, as in Ghana, the government instituted policy reforms favoring the agricultural sector, the immediate response in terms of increased export crops was striking.

As a result, however, of years of restriction of private sector activity, in many countries there now is real question as to whether and/or when the private sector in agriculture is capable of taking over the tasks that have been performed, albeit ineffectively, by the boards. The network of local traders that may have existed at independence has atrophied, and capital resources at the local level have seriously diminished. When Malawi decided in 1986 to return the maize trade to the private sector, there was some doubt whether enough private traders would or could pay the substantial licensing fee required to enter a field that had hitherto been the preserve of the government. Moreover, increased centralization of political and financial power in the hands of the national government has weakened local authorities to the point at which they have no longer been able to regulate local trading practices as they have in past.

Many governments quite correctly fear the political volatility of the cities, and continue to find it easier to control prices for food grains, subsidize the operating deficits of the marketing boards, and acquire needed additional supplies from external sources while selling them to the consumer at a profit above the concessional buying price than to face urban unrest. Returning agricultural marketing to private hands is dependent on the willingness of the government to engage in serious policy dialogue on changes that may appear to be only peripherally connected to agriculture. Unless these changes are made, however, agricultural trading will be less attractive to the private sector than other activities.

Moreover, as Killick and Commander (1988:1475) point out, because the variability of demand for agricultural inputs makes for such a high risk level and low profit, the state may have to offer incentives (say subsidies) to induce business to engage in the private supply of these inputs.

SPECIAL ASPECTS OF AGRICULTURAL PRIVATIZATION

Selling Agricultural Estates

With the changing attitudes of many LDC governments toward the agricultural sector, particularly the rise in prices paid to the producers, the question of privatizing agricultural estates owned and operated by government agencies has taken on new importance. Private sector operators now see greater possibility of profits from export and domestic crops with the liberalization of formerly controlled prices paid by the marketing boards. Many governments have discovered that private sector farms have become more productive and the crops are of a higher quality than was the case under state control.

Sales of large-scale government holding to private owners is not easy because of the limited availability of local capital, even if buyers with the necessary agricultural skills can be found. An effort was made to broaden ownership when Malawi set out to market large tea and macadamia nut estates, but it soon became apparent that few local individuals were able to finance the purchase of the largest estates. The only alternative was large external buyers, such as the Commonwealth Development Corporation.

A bilateral donor agency agreed to provide, out of the local currency equivalent of balance of payments support to the government, a cofinancing facility for estates of up to one thousand acres. The facility operated through a local commercial bank and loans were made up to 90 percent of the purchase price (as opposed to the bank's normal limit of 50 percent). Terms were extended as far as eight years. Few applications for financing were initially received because potential buyers were unaware of the facility, but now they are being encouraged to make use of it.

This use of donor funds could be replicated in other countries in which the government plans to divest large agriculural ventures. Since in most cases government marketing boards have neither the time nor the skills to devote to the day-to-day management of farm holdings, privatization will benefit not only the government but will probably result in higher production from the land. But little is accomplished if the sale benefits only large absentee landowners; a method has to be created for smaller farmers to take part in the sale by affording them special credit facilities.

Privatizing Land Ownership

Traditional land tenure practices in LDCs have frequently been an obstacle to the most effective utilization of land. In recent years attitudes toward possession of land are undergoing fundamental change, particularly in African countries. Hitherto the value of land has been in its usufruct, but ownership of the land itself had little or no intrinsic worth. Traditionally, ownership of land was vested in tribal authorities who possessed the power to grant use of parcels of land to individuals for subsistence production of food. With independence, overall ownership of land was often vested in the state. As the returns on food crops increase, land is rapidly becoming a source of profit and hence is being seen in an entirely new light as a form of personal wealth.

As a result, legal recognition of private ownership of land and judicial delineation of boundaries are becoming matters of critical importance. With the development of larger mining and agrobusiness projects, determination of the ownership or leasehold rights of the land to be used and its precise boundaries becomes necessary if the project is to go forward. In most African countries no registry of land ownership exists in rural areas. In urban areas, where extended families may be able to exert prior ownership claims, land development for industrial purposes may be subject to indefinite delay until all the claims can be sorted out in the courts.

Traditional law permitted neither sale of land nor its rental for profit; the land had to be used for the direct benefit of those living upon it. Now that land is beginning to have monetary value to its owners, governments are becoming more concerned with regulating the exchange of land and recognizing the rights of those already in possession of it. Those who believe in the statist theory of land ownership—that is, protection of the land for the ultimate use of the people in the face of the threat of alienation of large tracts to foreign control for exploitation of mineral or other resources or for industrial construction—and those who believe that private individuals should be free to acquire and sell land for profit as part of the liberalization of all economic activity are increasingly in debate.

Many governments are now approaching donors for assistance in developing land law and land registration procedures. In Guinea, for example, the World Bank and the Food and Agricultural Organization are considering cooperative assistance to create a system by which current land ownership can at least be identified and a limited registration scheme can be set up. Full land registration is beyond the administrative capacities of most African governments and would be prohibitively costly to maintain at the local governmental level.

The Ugandan government has requested help in identifying Indian owners of lands and businesses nationalized in 1972 when the original owners were expelled. Although the government's expressed intention is to repay the original owners for their losses, the more important point is that, without clear title, the present African occupiers of the properties are not prepared to invest in improvements.

McLindon (1989:17) has reported that in the Senegal River Valley in Senegal the complex land tenure system is seen as a constraint to private sector development by large landowners. Recent dam construction has made newly irrigated land more attractive, and substantial numbers of requests are being received by local authorities for additional allocations. These are, however, running into resistance from traditional elites, who seek to continue their control over the land rather than distribute it to the landless. Land cannot be mortgaged to finance new acquisition nor can it be sold, purchased, or leased. It has been recommended that the government adopt a system of land registration according to standardized recording and mapping practices. Pressure for development of leasing arrangements and means to facilitate land transfers is also growing as the price of paddy rice becomes more attractive.

Use of technical assistance to allow LDC governments to create formal land registration agencies and develop laws for the sale and lease of private property would be welcomed in several countries. It would meet a growing need in supporting private sector growth as well as emphasizing the advantages of privatization.

Experiments in Agricultural Privatization

Despite the difficulty in replacing the functions of the marketing boards, countries in Asia, Africa, and Latin America have tried, with varying success, a number of experiments to privatize aspects of the agricultural sector.

- *Bangladesh*. Privatization of fertilizer distribution has been proceeding slowly. This particular commodity lends itself very well to private distribution. The government usually acts as the bulk buyer, while distribution can be turned over to private traders who sell directly to the consumer at officially fixed prices, allowing for reasonable profit. With donor assistance privatization of fertilizer distribution is being developed in Cameroon.

- *Pakistan*. Private tube wells in the Indus River Plain now outnumber similar wells constructed by the government, and it is anticipated that private wells built by individuals or groups of farmers will replace government-owned wells.

- *The Philippines*. The government is seeking with donor assistance to privatize agrobusiness and agrimarketing firms such as the National Food Authority and commodity firms such as the Philippine Cotton, Dairy, and Tobacco Corporations.

- *Sri Lanka and Thailand*. Controls over rice have been liberalized and the seed industry is being recommended for transfer to the private sector.

- *Mali*. A new role for the private sector has been initiated by the government with the coordinated assistance of external donors. In 1980 it was agreed that the marketing of cereal grains would be put in private hands and the operations of the agricultural marketing board, OPAM, would undergo gradual reform over a period of six years. During this time the cereals market would be restructured and the board would function only as a coordinator of sales rather than as a direct buyer from the producer, except that in a food crisis, the board reserved the power to become the buyer and seller of last resort. Subsidies were not entirely eliminated. The donors' collectively pledged to supply food grains at concessional prices and the local currency thus generated would be used for a declining subsidy over the six year period of the agreement. It would appear that the private sector is gaining strength through the trial period and the board has confined itself largely to a coordinating role.

• *Guinea*. The military government that succeeded the regime of Sékou Touré made a number of moves to liberalize the agricultural trade that was formerly entirely in government hands. State farms have been eliminated and the land has been returned to private farmers, with a resulting increase in coffee and rice production. Four SOEs in the field of agricultural inputs and cash crop exports are in the process of being closed. However, opportunities for private sector investment in agriculture outside of trade still remain limited.

• *Nigeria*. The government decided in April 1986 to eliminate by the end of that year all six commodity marketing boards and turn their functions over to the private sector. Government intervention in agriculture went back to 1942, but the marketing board system (covering cocoa, groundnuts, cotton, rubber, grain, and palm products) dated from 1977. The boards had almost complete power over trading in those commodities and operated with a staff of over 30,000. In addition, it was announced that eleven government-owned companies concerned directly with agriculture would be privatized because it was considered that on balance they were costly and inefficient and acted more as a deterrent to agricultural development than as a help.

In the abrupt abolition of the boards, little thought was given to whether the private sector had the capacity to take over the boards' functions immediately. No transitional arrangements were provided in the decree abolishing the boards, and foreign buyers questioned whether the private sector would be able to exert sufficient quality control over export commodities. To ensure the quality of export shipments, the government ultimately decided to make export licenses issued to private traders conditional on production of a federal produce inspection certificate. Without close supervision, however, this licensing system could lead to corrupt practices.

• *Senegal*. The government plans to reduce nonproductive agencies in agriculture. Fertilizer distribution has been privatized. State control of cereals marketing has been abolished; regional agricultural parastatals are now involved chiefly with the provision of extension services.

• *Zimbabwe*. The government has proved conclusively that price incentives can increase agricultural production. By raising the prices paid to farmers for cereals by 50 percent, production by African as well as European farmers doubled in one year to the point where existing storage facilities became insufficient.

• *Malawi*. The government has embarked on a program of placing the marketing of maize grown by small farmers in the hands of licensed private traders, with the agricultural marketing board remaining as the buyer of last resort.

• *Swaziland*. A new firm, Commercial Agricultural Production and Marketing, will provide direct and indirect assistance to private sector firms expanding input services to the agricultural sector.

• *Chile*. An attempt has been made to privatize agricultural extension services to small holders. Specialists chosen from a government-approved list were provided to give advice to farmers. They were paid partly by the farmer and partly by government subsidy, with the work being supervised by the government.

• *Eastern Caribbean states*. American companies are interested in taking over citrus juice operations now owned by the government, and in Belize a banana marketing operation has been privatized with donor help.

TECHNIQUES FOR ENCOURAGING AGRICULTURAL PRIVATIZATION

Agricultural policy has been the subject of intense review by both governments and lending agencies, largely in the context of broader policy dialogue dealing with reduction of the role of the public sector. As the results of these reviews become available, governments are becoming more inclined to adopt reform measures, as the Nigerian and Malian examples prove.

Agricultural privatization remains, however, an exceedingly sensitive political area in most LDCs. Vested interests in the bureaucracy and in the political arena are likely to be endangered by any moves to reduce the role of entrenched marketing boards. Stubborn resistance can be expected, particularly from those whose jobs are threatened. But when it comes to balancing interest group opposition with producing enough food for the urban areas by increasing incentives to the farmers, governments are likely to turn a more receptive ear to reform initiatives. A full understanding is needed of the political ramifications entailed by drastic reduction of the role of marketing boards or their total elimination before donors embark on an assistance program.

Any changes that are made in macroeconomic policy will have little effect if they are not accompanied by price incentives to the producer. Peasant farmers are not unaware of world prices, and without equitable return on their export crops or fair prices for food grains, they will simply cease production or switch to a barter economy. In Tanzania, for example, failure by the government marketing agencies to provide adequate return or provide means by which commercial crops could be brought to market caused many peasants to revert to subsistence farming. Since 1986, the government has instituted policy changes in food crop marketing aimed at legitimizing the role of private traders. Transportation has been a major constraint to agricultural inputs and marketing of domestic and export crops, and the government has sought to increase private sector participation in the movement of food crops.

It may be necessary to put together an inventory of the capacities of the private sector to replace marketing board functions prior to advancing a privatization plan. If the trading community is not large enough to service the producers or if the transport network cannot be relied upon to get agricultural production to market, privatizing may not be effective. Donors will need to coordinate privatization plans for agriculture with other projects in this sector, such as rural transportation or provision of rural credit facilities.

The overall economic environment in which agriculture operates has to be taken into account. Persuading the government to increase producer prices will not have the desired result if inflation or consumer goods shortages make it impossible for farmers to buy what they want with increased income from the incentive of higher prices for their production. Policy dialogue on macroeconomic changes is an integral part of agricultural privatization.

The government's views on large scale foreign or joint venture private sector agrobusiness must be taken into account. Such ventures may increase production, particularly of export crops, but they may at the same time create a political backlash if large numbers of individual farmers are displaced.

Privatization of the agricultural sector is just as important and just as possible as it is in the industrial sector. It requires different techniques and a sensitive approach; it may be slower and require even more patience than selling industrial units. Partial privatization may have to be accepted as an initial step. A government agency may have to remain, at least temporarily, as the importer of a major agricultural input, such as fertilizer, while domestic distribution is given over to the private sector. But privatization in this sector may ultimately have more profound effects on the society as a whole than divestment of state-owned enterprises, particularly in those LDCs in which agriculture remains the major form of economic activity.

6

The Future of Privatization in the Developing World

It has been argued in both the industrialized and the developing world that the current interest and activity in privatization is a temporary phenomenon, stemming from advocacy by the United States government, in particular, and from pressures exerted by the international lending agencies to reduce third world deficits by increasing the efficiency of the public sector. Although ideology undoubtedly played some role initially in Western donors' encouragement of privatization efforts in the LDCs, based in part on the experience of private sector success in their own histories, privatization has taken on a life of its own in the developing world that has much more to do with the practical requirements of governing the state than with ideological conviction.

Successful privatizations in the United Kingdom and Western Europe have been cited as evidence that privatization can reduce subsidy costs and increase the productivity of formerly state-owned enterprises. It has also been demonstrated that privatizing by means of stock offerings provides an opportunity to introduce many thousands of new shareholders in the developing world to the financial operations that are part and parcel of a modern industrialized economy.

The ideology that, in part, prompted the expansion of state control over the economy in many LDCs in the immediate post-independence period is gradually being succeeded by a more pragmatic approach to development based on a search for effective solutions to the critical economic problems of the developing world. By the end of two decades of independence it became clear that many states failed to achieve their goals within a totally planned economy, and the conviction grew that governments were simply unable to carry out effectively many economic activities. The combination of falling commodity prices, higher energy costs, and mounting debt charges made more urgent the search for an alternative approach to development in which the private sector would play a substantially more important role than in the past. This view is shared by more and more of the younger postnationalist generation of politicians and civil servants, who are now rising to positions of power and influence in LDC governments, and is symbolized by the privatization of SOEs.

It was always clear, of course, that there would continue to be a role for the state in supplying goods and services that the private sector would have neither the capacity nor the interest to undertake. The problem faced by governments, and indeed donors as well, is how best to achieve the most acceptable and effective mix between state and private sector activities in view of the varying capacity of the private sector in each country to play a larger part in industrial and agricultural production.

THE POSITIVE RESULTS OF PRIVATIZATION

While it is too soon to make broad judgments about the effect of privatization programs on LDC economies generally, positive results are already becoming evident in a growing number of countries. In Central America and the Caribbean, banks, telecommunications facilities, industries, and agricultural projects have been put in private hands with good results for the investors. The Mexican government has reduced the number of SOEs by 75 percent, from twelve hundred to three hundred firms, either by sale or dissolution. In Ghana, policy reforms aimed at providing new export incentives and higher prices for farmers brought a 50 percent increase in agricultural exports in one year. Elimination of commodity marketing boards in Nigeria produced a similar result. In southern Africa, liberalization of agricultural policies by placing marketing activities and inputs in private hands is bringing in both new foreign investors and increasing farm productivity. In Southeast Asia privatization programs have been slow to develop, except in Malaysia, which is providing an example for neighboring Thailand and Indonesia through its privatization of port facilities, the national airline, and communication facilities. It has been asserted that the number of privatizations between 1983 and 1988 in the developing world "is rapidly approaching 1,000" (Nellis and Kikeri, 1989:668).

Apart from strengthening the productive capabilities of industry and agriculture, privatization will have ancillary effects on other aspects of the economy.

With the growth of the private sector in LDCs as a result of privatizations and new investment, there has emerged a corresponding need for a modernized banking and financial system capable of offering long-term credit and dealing with sophisticated financial instruments. In most LDCs commercial banks have not played a leading role in financing privatization because they have been unwilling to assume more than short-term risk. Without readily available sources of credit, many potential local buyers will be unable to take advantage of privatization opportunities.

Privatization and new private sector ventures have also radically increased the number of first time shreholders in many LDCs. The demand for banks to handle stock transactions and other profitable investor services, such as dividend collection, will be increasing rapidly, as will the knowledge of the use of banks as agents spreads.

Many LDCs see the existence of a stock market as a prerequisite to financial modernization. Successful privatization does not necessarily depend on this, however, as the many sales of SOEs to individuals and joint partnerships demonstrate. Operation of a stock market requires trained personnel, complex regulation by the government, some degree of sophistication on the part of investors, and a variety of offerings from which buyers may choose. While privatizations may provide new offerings, the task of marketing them falls to brokers who themselves have to acquire experience. In any case, LDC stock markets are far from being a factor in the international capital market; their total capitalization is only slightly over 3 percent of the New York Stock Exchange alone. New financial instruments and donor-assisted training of market specialists will encourage market growth, but even under the most favorable conditions, it will be a slow process and will be dependent on the growing strength of the private sector.

A successful privatization program does not depend on having a stock market, as many sales to individuals and joint partnerships demonstrate. But, if an active market already exists, it may rapidly become a vehicle for successful privatizations that in turn strengthen the market itself, as the case of Nigeria illustrates. The Nigerian privatization program was started in mid-1988 with the announcement that ninety-two enterprises were to be privatized, sixty-seven of them by full divestment of government ownership. Some fifty enterprises were to be sold by stock offering on the Nigerian exchange. By late 1989, four public offerings had been made with twelve more to follow early in the new year.

With a program of this magnitude, it was feared that the absorptive capacity of the capital market might be strained, but all three of the first offerings were oversubscribed by substantial margins. Nigerian critics of privatization argued that divestment would only serve to further enrich those with wealth enough to buy shares, but this idea was negated by the fact that over 75 percent of the shares sold were to applicants seeking between two hundred and one thousand shares. It is estimated that the privatizations completed thus far have created over 300,000 new shareholders. Commenting on the success of the divestment program, the director of the technical committee overseeing its implementation said, ''What we are witnessing is a silent revolution in the corporate ownership structure of productive investments in the national economy. To those who saw privatization as a transfer of public property to a few rich people, the message is loud and clear, that it is not. It is in fact a program of mass participation of popular capitalism'' (Zayyad, 1989:21).

The Nigerian program contains a feature that is likely to be found in future privatization programs elsewhere. Provision is made for state-owned enterprises to become ''commercialized,'' that is, to become self-sufficient in both recurrent and capital expenditure by more efficient, profit-oriented management. Profits from ''commercialized'' firms will be returned to the Treasury, and additional capital for expansion will be raised on the capital market. In effect, commercialization means that such SOEs would be operated as though they were privately owned, although the government retains full ownership. While it can be argued that this is not privatization in the real sense of the word, it may well lead to sale of the firm at a later point if commercialization produces a profitable enterprise.

A further ancillary benefit to be derived from privatizing is the expanded growth of a skilled entrepreneurial group. With privatization comes opportunities for new economic activities and training for new skills. Industries formerly run by the state come into private hands with accompanying needs for greater managerial abilities and a trained work force. Small entrepreneurs begin to establish firms in competition with SOEs, which, if they are successful, may eliminate the need for industries operated by the state and force them out of business.

THE CRITICS OF PRIVATIZATION

Despite its advantages, privatization is not without its critics. As a remedy for the economic problems of governments in the developing world, it has vocal opponents in both the public and private sectors. It has been contended that the large-scale privatization of the United Kingdom, for example, has limited applicability to the developing world in the absence of the instruments, techniques, and financial skills that made it possible in an industrialized country. Nor is the substantial investment capital available in Europe to be found in the LDCs. Where some local private capital is to be found, a choice must be made between utilizing it to buy SOEs and creating new enterprises for which there may be greater need or that may be more attractive as investment opportunities.

The point has been made that the turn to privatization is a reflection of a change in the value structure of Western democracies that is not necessarily transferable to developing countries. The Western desire to improve the efficiency of resource use by shifting the productive sector of the economy from state to private hands loses sight, it is claimed, of the need for equality of treatment in economic advance for all members of society. Killick and Commander (1988:1465–66) argue, "It is common for public enterprises to be used as a means of subsidizing consumers, for example, for wage goods or the delivery of economic services. The substitution of market-determined prices for previously subsidized prices will create a group of unambiguous losers." This point has been made by several developing world leaders, as it relates to structural adjustment lending as well as to privatization. Killick and Commander add, however, "These [the losers] may or may not be made up of poverty groups, for state subsidies are a notoriously inefficient way of alleviating poverty. Subsidies tend to have a strong urban bias and even in a rural economy a disproportionate share of the benefits is liable to be captured by local elites" (1466).

Part of the case against privatizing has its source in the colonial history of the developing world. It is maintained (*West Africa*, May 1988:823) that "the nationalization of foreign-owned companies at independence was not just an assertion of nationalism; it was also necessary to gain control of the economy which had previously been determined by needs that were mostly at variance with the aspirations of the people." The pressures exerted on LDC governments to rely more heavily on free market forces and private sector initiative do not, it is contended, take into account that the private sector suffers from the same faults of which the state has been accused. The *West Africa* article continues:

The privatization argument ... ignores the important fact that public ownership was in many cases prompted by failure of the market and the effective absence of willing and compatible private agents. ... On the whole there is no guarantee that the relatively underdeveloped private sector in Africa can increase efficiency or lead to less corruption. ... The current trend towards privatization could at best be temporarily shelving the problem of nation-building that African countries have been engaged in (823).

A similar note of skepticism has been sounded in a report of the UN's Economic Commission for Africa, which argues that privatization in Africa, at the present time at least, is impossible because the private sector is simply not capable of taking over the functions now performed by SOEs. Moreover, the policy reforms leading to market-controlled prices demanded by structural adjustment lending and privatization will result in increased poverty at the lower end of the social scale, while serving to enrich the new entrepreneurs that are a result of them. This may in some degree be true if the reforms further skew the distribution of wealth in societies in which incomes are already in imbalance. It might be countered, however, that limitations on spending for government delivery of services that arise from the necessity to pay subsidy costs of state ownership of productive resources are already affecting the poor in many countries. Higher government revenues resulting from taxation of profitiable private sector enterprises would allow for needed expansion of services to the poorest sectors of the population, provided the government is prepared to enforce redistribution of wealth through a stringent system of tax levies on personal income.

The claims that large-scale privatization will have serious effects on the poorer groups in society because they will have to pay more for electric power and transportation and consumer goods from privately owned industries must be taken seriously if for no other reason than that they have political consequences. Apart from the predicted increase in poverty (the case for which has yet to be proved), there are groups in LDC societies that stand to lose prestige and position if the state relinquishes control over large SOEs. Divestment will initially create labor redundancy, and where unemployment poses a serious urban problem, the government will have to consider the short-term unrest that may result from it. It is encumbent on the government to demonstrate that privately owned firms can assume responsibility for the role now played by SOEs and that, as the private sector grows, new opportunities for employment and investment will be created. This will take time because the restructuring and privatization of industries is a complicated, and often disturbing, process, not only in the developing world but, as the Soviet and Eastern European governments are also beginning to discover with their new interest in privatizing, in the socialist world as well.

THE FUTURE FOR PRIVATIZATION

The first decade of privatization has been largely a matter of learning and experimenting in the developing world. The concept in itself was revolutionary, the process had to be adapted to the special needs of less developed countries, and the results are only now beginning to show. Many governments seized upon privatization as the panacea that would solve all their economic ills—money losing SOEs would be sold to the highest bidder, profitable firms would be retained for their contribution to development, and receipts from the sales would go to balance the budget. Unfortunately, privatizing proved to be much more complex than expected—at best, it was slow and frustrating. Governments learned too that it was not carried out in a vacuum; successful privatization meant facing often unwelcome decisions for macroeconomic policy change.

One of the most important lessons of the past decade has been that privatization is just one instrument among many that must be employed if economic recovery is to be achieved. The responsibility for greater efficiency and higher production must be shared by both the private and the public sectors; the problem is how best to mix these sectors so that the welfare of both the individual and the society can be most effectively advanced.

Once begun, privatization cannot be easily reversed. If it succeeds, a popular constituency for it is created. Unless a new regime is prepared to renationalize profitable privatized industries without compensation to the new owners, the cost of returning them to state control will be greater than the government can afford. On the other hand, if privatized firms are mismanaged, are unable to meet the costs of technological modernization, or are buffeted by external market conditions, the government may feel pressured to take them over at a cost to the taxpayer just to maintain employment and production.

LDC governments have gradually become more comfortable with privatization because they more fully appreciate that by divestment they do not lose control of development. The power to regulate is only now being more fully understood; judicious use of it without impeding private initiative will provide the government with enough control to give direction to development without itself becoming immediately involved.

There is increasing evidence that future privatization will concentrate more on services and agriculture than largely on industry as has been the case hitherto. Governments are becoming more aware of their limitations in providing the high quality services that are now in demand and are beginning to show greater inclination to entrust these services, in part at least, to the private sector. The greatest advances in this field will probably appear first in the health sector, but with time they will spread through most fields of service delivery.

As governments gain experience with privatization, the techniques will become more refined and new methods of financing will make divestment easier and quicker. More widespread knowledge of privatizing methods as they have been applied in the developing world will tend to decrease reliance on European models that have up to now often been less than satisfactory. Third world countries, such as Malaysia, will be able to provide the expertise that has been the province of Western advisors in the early years of privatization. Advice and technical assistance from developing country experts, who are more apt to have a fuller understanding of the peculiar difficulties an LDC will face in privatizing, will serve to increase the confidence of governments embarked on divestment for the first time.

Privatizing is only one of many routes to greater prosperity in the developing world but it is central to freeing the LDCs from the economic disasters so many have experienced in the past decade. It can help to rejuvenate the tarnished dream of national development through industrialization that was the goal of so many of the early nationalist leaders of Asia and Africa. At the same time it can help to realize the new dream of individual independence in a modern society that is becoming the goal of the current generation in the developing world.

Appendix: Case Histories in Privatization in the LDCs

The case histories that follow are designed to illustrate how some of the techniques of privatization have been applied in actual divestment situations in selected LDCs. They range from sale of a bank to divestment of agricultural estates and from direct sale to individuals to sale by large stock offerings.

Drawn by permission from the files of the United States Agency for International Development, these cases illustrate the variety of ways in which a bilateral donor can assist in planning and preparation of a privatization program. The contribution of A.I.D. missions includes advice on how to prepare an SOE for divestment, buyer search, financing, institutional change, and dialogue designed to lead to macroeconomic policy change. The cases provide concrete examples of how privatization works in the field and how difficulties relating to program development and execution have been overcome.

JAMAICA: ADDRESSING POLITICAL FACTORS IN PRIVATIZING: THE NATIONAL COMMERCIAL BANK AND THE CARIBBEAN CEMENT COMPANY

Introduction

The Jamaican government has embarked over the past six years on one of the most extensive privatization programs to be found anywhere in the developing world. A divestment committee was established in 1981 to provide the technical information to the political leadership on firms to be divested.

Divestment efforts covered a wide variety of SOEs including major divestitures (such as the National Commercial Bank and the Caribbean Cement Co.), leasing of land through the A.I.D. sponsored Agro-21 Project, the sale and lease of hotels, privatization of a number of smaller enterprises by private share placement, and, most recently, privatization of the telephone system. One of the early placements in the program was SEPROD Limited, a group of companies in consumer products and animal feeds that was sold in 1985 by a private share placement of $J30 million combined with a public share offering of $J8 million, the first such offering since 1973. This successful venture proved that the Jamaican private sector could be utilized in subsequent privatizations.

Privatizing the National Commercial Bank (NCB)

The privatization of 51 percent of NCB shares in December 1986 was Jamaica's first exercise in major share offering. The 30.6 million shares were sold for $J90 million. Some thirty thousand new shareholders were created and 84 million shares were applied for—an oversubscription of 175 percent. (An account of the technical aspects of the privatization is to be found in Leeds, 1987a).

There was surprisingly little political opposition to the sale of NCB, compared to what might have been expected, given the political history of Jamaica over the past twenty years. The national political spectrum is based on two parties, the Peoples' National party (PNP), led by Michael Manley, and the Jamaica Labor party (JLP), led by Edward Seaga. The PNP, which had been in power prior to 1980, espoused a socialist program. Many of the intellectuals supporting the PNP are graduates of the London School of Economics. While in power, Manley's government had increased the role of the state in the economy with a number of nationalizations, including the NCB. By the end of the 1970s there were over two hundred SOEs, accounting for 20 percent of GDP. Most were money losers; the SOEs' deficit increased from 4 percent of GDP in 1971 to 18 percent in 1980.

Although the PNP was officially opposed to privatizing because, the party argued, it would lead to sale of the national patrimony to wealthy individuals and to foreigners, the party had itself engaged in a form of privatizing in the 1970s by disposing of idle state-owned sugar-growing land to cooperatives. This was seen as being in the interests of popular control of the means of production. The experiment was largely a disaster because of the failure of the coops to manage the new lands. As a result, the government became involved again in state farming.

Edward Seaga's campaign in 1980 was based on seeking "a new foundation for Jamaica's economic growth" and on opposition to the perceived socialism of the PNP. The new foundation was to include a substantial role for the private sector; democratization of ownership would be achieved by public offerings of shares in the industries owned by the state. It was expected that successful privatization would create political support for the JLP from those who would benefit from their new holdings. It was essential, then, in choosing a candidate for privatization that there be the prospect of an immediate increase in share prices to create the new political constituency. The choice of NCB for privatization was a particularly happy one from a political viewpoint for a number of reasons:

- NCB was one of the few profitable state enterprises.
- NCB was a well-known institution to many Jamaicans who had dealt with it through its branches throughout the country. The public had confidence in the bank's future and was comfortable with the idea of owning shares in it.
- The scheme for the sale of shares attracted labor leaders, who were consulted about the sale from the outset.
- NCB had a very loyal staff of eighteen hundred, who were not only prepared to buy shares but cooperated in the sale by distributing and accepting application forms at all branches.

Initially, the PNP was strongly opposed to the offering, branding it as an ideological aggression and accusing the U.S. ambassador of meddling in Jamaican affairs since the U.S.A.I.D. mission was providing technical assistance. However, as the educational campaign on privatizing the bank progressed, the opposition's tone grew less vitriolic as it became clear that the offering, partly because of the NCB's excellent record of community relations, was widely popular. The opposition's hope for an ideological battle over the issue became less and less realistic.

The government made a conspicuous effort to consult with the opposition leadership to make sure that the PNP was fully informed about the details of the sale. Manley, a former official of his cabinet, and a high party official were invited to meet with the majority party leadership to raise any question they felt necessary.

A well-thought-out and intensive publicity campaign was mounted by the Jamaican Information Service to acquaint prospective buyers with the meaning of owning shares. Full page newspaper advertisements were used repeatedly to build up popular enthusiasm for the offer, and radio and television programs extolled the virtues of share ownership. Question and answer sessions were featured on radio talk shows; to avoid legal inaccuracies all published answers to questions were checked with lawyers beforehand. The theme of shares growing in value, as would an agricultural crop, was strongly stressed. In addition, the point was made that the shares could be used as collateral, emphasizing particularly that dividends could be used to provide savings to build a house.

Briefing sessions were held with all interested groups, ranging from employers associations to labor leaders, in an attempt to defuse the opposition attacks. As the campaign grew more intensive with the approaching sale, trade unionists began to realize that opposition could mean a rank and file backlash. In general, labor redundancy has not been a major objection to privatization in Jamaica, and in the case of the NCB, staffing was tight enough that there was little prospect of any loss of jobs with private sector control, particularly if employees were to become owners of a substantial part of the shares.

The opposition's tone grew markedly less strident after the visit by Neal Kinnoch, leader of the British Labor party, to Jamaica shortly before the offering. He apparently advised the PNP that further opposition could be counterproductive and make the party look like a spoilsport in the face of the sale's general acceptance. The government stressed the theme that mass ownership was the road to economic democracy; and the opposition found it hard to counter the argument. The point of handing over control to a few individuals, Jamaican or foreign, was blunted by the limitation that no more that 7.5 percent of the shares could be held by any one person or institution. This was rigidly adhered to in the sale process.

After the initial sale offering to the public at $J2.95 in October 1986, NCB stock promptly climbed to over $J4.00 a share, partially as a result of deliberate underpricing by the underwriters and partially because of the stock's scarcity value. It later sank to a normal trading range of $J3.50 to $J4.50. Those who bought shares under the complicated allocation scheme of the opening offer were, needless to say, highly satisfied with their purchase and, indeed, many individuals wished they had bought more.

The evident success of the offering, with its heavy oversubscription, left the opposition with a short ideological leg to stand on. In the end, political opposition to the 51 percent privatization of the NCB's shares was largely ineffectual, and the case was further weakened by the immediate rise in the price of the stock. The opposition made clear, however, that any further disposal of the remaining 49 percent would be opposed. Nevertheless, the government made no secret of its intention to divest the remaining shares at some future point, depending on market strength.

The remaining 49 percent of NCB's shares continued to be held by the National Investment Bank of Jamaica (NIBJ). The government remained determined to carry out its expressed intention of complete divestment. In March 1988 the offering was finally made, but the results were not exactly what the government had expected.

The decision to make the offering had in fact been taken some months earlier, but its execution was delayed by depressed world market conditions following the fall of the U.S. market in October 1987. The government's financial advisers judged that conditions were improving to the point at which the offering could be made public, and the government was anxious to go ahead in view of the forthcoming elections due in a few months.

The offering was not, however, made in the same form as the previously successful public participation sale. Instead, it was to be by tender offer, limited to institutions such as banks, pension funds, mutual funds, and building societies. The same ownership limitations were to apply—a maximum of 7.5 percent of the stock in the hands of any individual or firm. The government's reason for this type of offer stemmed in part from complaints made by financial houses that, because of the popularity of the initial issue, applications by institutions had been severely scaled back to accommodate the demand by individual buyers. To provide greater flexibility in NCB management, the government was interested in increasing the number of shareholders with substantial blocks of stock. Accordingly, the offer was made privately to twenty-eight institutions, each of which was allowed to make up to five bids at five different prices.

The timing of the offer was critical; it had to be open long enough for bids to be prepared and submitted but not so long that bidders would have the opportunity for collusion on their bids. Since the Jamaican stock market is open only on Tuesday and Thursday afternoons, the offer was opened on Thursday after the close of the market and bids were to be returned by the following Tuesday morning prior to the market opening later in the day.

In setting its close scheduling for the second offer, however, the government underestimated the collusive skills of the Jamaican business community. When bids were opened they ranged from $J2.70 to $J4.25, with two-thirds of them under $J3.30, substantially below the current market price. The striking absence of bids above $J3.30 roused strong suspicion that there had been considerable communication among potential bidders over the weekend. Indeed, there was a rumor that the government had gotten wind of the bidding trend from disgruntled bidders not included in the low-bidders group and realized what was happening.

Institutions were attempting to buy the stock at a substantial discount, assuming that a bargain could be had because the government was badly in need of funds to redress upcoming budget shortages. Some of the bidders argued, however, that collusion had never taken place; rather the bids were based on a correct analysis of the value of NCB stock. They claimed that at $J3.30, the trend in the stock was down and a bid of $J2.70 to $J2.90 was simply a realistic appraisal of the future value of the stock. It would appear, however, that this was rather too simplistic an explanation for the curious range of bids submitted.

In any case, the NIBJ chairman was quoted as saying there was evidence that "a number of institutions had attempted to act in concert," and the government promptly withdrew the offer. To have done otherwise would have been to court political disaster by exposing the government to the charge that it was prepared to sell the stock at discounted prices to favored business interests. It would have played directly into hands of the PNP, which had earlier indicated its objection to further divestment of NCB shares.

The net effect of the whole effort was to drive down NCB stock to a low of $J3.50. Journalists promptly reminded the public that the real losers were NCB and its current shareholders. Under the circumstances, it was highly unlikely that the government would risk attempting to sell NIBJ's shares in the NCB again before the election. After the withdrawal of the sale offer, the PNP made a statement to the press that "if the JLP Administration carries through this act of betrayal, a future PNP government would have no option but to take appropriate action to right this wrong" (*Kingston Daily Gleaner*, March 18, 1988, p. 1).

Seaga's government immediately attacked the statement. In the legislature, he responded to the opposition "threats" saying:

We have heard various threats being made out of two sides of the same mouth. In one breath, the voice supports the divestment. In another breath, we are told that it is a sale of the national patrimony and we are constantly being barraged by threats of what another party will do if it becomes the government. Let me here announce that, if any other party becomes the government of this country, it is powerless to reverse this process. I go further and say it is absolutely powerless to reverse this process. (*Kingston Daily Gleaner*, March 19, 1988, p. 1).

He went on to "enlighten the ignorant" that in the case of the NCB, the memorandum of Articles of Association of the bank under divestment were drawn up in a manner so that 90 percent of the shareholders was required to form a quorum who must all agree to increase the ownership limitation beyond 7.5 percent. And so, he concluded, "Unless 90 percent of all persons owning NCB shares . . . meet in the National Stadium and by 100 percent vote decide that they want the government to become a shareholder which goes beyond the 7.5 percent, no power on earth can change that [limit], save you tear up the Constitution and throw it away" (*Kingston Daily Gleaner*, March 19, 1988, p. 1).

Despite these strong statements on both sides, the reality of the situation is that a reversal of the initial NCB sale through renationalization is extremely unlikely. The number of those holding shares in Jamaican companies increased from three thousand to over thirty-three thousand with the NCB sale. An additional eight thousand shareholders were added with the Caribbean Cement Company divestment. Such a constituency cannot be ignored, particularly since the shares have appreciated in value. Moreover, as some commentators have pointed out, however much the PNP may wish to increase the level of social services, there is little prospect that this can be accomplished, unless the country earns more or goes further into debt. Seaga is faced with the same scenario; more services can only be provided by higher borrowing.

The argument was made by some executives in the financial community that the government made a basic policy error in deciding to carry out the sale of the remaining shares by restricted tender bid, regardless of the weakness in world stock prices. Some blamed it on the government's immediate need for money (although it appears that this was a misperception since the fiscal year ended with a deficit of less than 1 percent). Others blamed the same British financial advisers who had successfully advised on the earlier sale, claiming that no foreigner could ever really understand the close relationships that existed within the relatively closed Jamaican financial community. There may be some basis for this, but it can be exaggerated; the advice of British investment bankers was in good part responsible for the successful offering in the first place.

According to some of the government's critics, a public offering on the same basis as the earlier one would have been successful, from both a financial and a political viewpoint. The earlier offering, they pointed out, was oversubscribed by $J160 million, more than enough to have sold 100 percent of NCB shares at $J2.95. There was at least some prospect that enough unsatisfied buyers remained to have carried out a second sale, thereby creating additional satisfied shareholders. On the other hand, market conditions were not as propitious in early 1988, and the sale price would have had to at least equal the current market price of NCB shares or the previous buyers would have objected strongly.

The government's objective in tender bidding was motivated in part by the consideration that too great a fragmentation in share ownership was undesirable, since it effectively left control of the NCB in the hands of management and the employees who collectively owned a substantial block of shares. Individual shareholdings were not large enough to influence management decisions, and unless they were organized, shareholders would be unlikely to elect representative directors to the board. Allowing financial institutions to hold 7.5 percent of the shares would at least permit the choice of experienced directors if the institutions could agree to vote as a bloc on who might represent them. The NCB's chief executive indicated that he favored this method of securing directors who would be able to offer expert advice on management questions and exercise greater check over management actions.

Privatizing the Caribbean Cement Company (CCC)

The CCC, 99.4 percent owned by government, has had a checkered history. It lost money in more years than it was profitable and paid no dividends since 1976. The government took a substantial risk when, in June 1987 the decision was made to place 100 percent of its shares on the market, since they were in large degree a speculative investment. Under these circumstances, the sale of eighty-nine million shares at $J2.00 per share was an impressive showing. Over twenty-four thousand applications were made, including those from 99 percent of the company's 450 employees. Nevertheless, only 72 percent of the total share capital was sold, in part a reflection of (1) a depressed stock market, (2) the recent issue of a government bond that sopped up liquidity, and (3) the thinness of the Jamaican capital market.

Part of the failure to sell the entire offering may also be due to the outspoken opposition of the PNP. The party termed the CCC privatization "a sordid transaction" and condemned it as doing "a great injustice to the Jamaican consumer and tax payer by transferring at discount prices the benefits to a few investors and speculators" (Cited in Leeds, 1987:52–53).

It is difficult to say with any certainty that the PNP's position was a serious deterrent to prospective buyers; several Jamaican financial officers expressed doubts that politics was a major factor in the shortfall in sales. It is more likely that the past record of the company discouraged some buyers and that the interval between the NCB and CCC offerings was too short given the thin capital market— there was just not enough disposable savings in the hands of small buyers to purchase additional shares.

Lessons from the Jamaican Experience

The limited Jamaican experience thus far would indicate that, partly as a result of the public education campaign by the government, the political opposition did not make any serious difference in the success of the privatizations. Although the PNP's position was well known, its ideological appeal did not overcome the prospect of profit from buying shares. There is no doubt that politics played an indirect role in that the issue served the purposes of the PNP as a weapon to attack the government in the legislature and gave the party a certain amount of free publicity in the process.

As a national issue, opposition arguments were of little long-range value, since any arguments against participation in buying shares fell on deaf ears once the share prices abruptly rose. The opposition realized that it was doing its own cause more harm than good in threatening renationalization. In the case of the CCC, the PNP's vituperative statements were almost pro forma, and they appeared to have little effect.

The Jamaican case illustrates two fundamental prerequisites in blunting political opposition to privatization. First, preliminary consultation with interest groups, particularly labor, paid off handsomely. Moreover, formal consultation with prominent opposition political leaders before the divestiture impressed on them that the government was concerned with hearing their point of view.

The skillful use of the mass media to explain stockholding, share purchase, and the potential uses of future dividend payments created a groundswell of popular support that the opposition could not overcome with theoretical argument. Careful and thorough preparation of the public may do more in the long run to ensure the success of a privatization than any amount of strategic planning confined only to government circles.

COSTA RICA: POLITICS AND PRIVATIZING CODESA

Introduction

Privatization has been of interest to the government of Costa Rica for several years. It is strongly supported by the president and the ruling National Liberation party. It has been assisted by the A.I.D. mission since the outset.

The Costa Rican political system is based on a weak presidential office with a strong legislature that has substantial power of decision. Despite these obstacles, President Arias has been able to overcome legislative opposition to privatization actions for seven companies, which constitute 90 percent of the holding company for state enterprises, CODESA.

The A.I.D. mission played a vital role in getting the privatization process under way. A principal supporter within the government was the Central Bank, which was highly conscious of the losses being suffered by the larger state-owned enterprises. In 1983–84, these enterprises were absorbing one-third of public sector credit to cover operating losses.

Objections to privatization were centered in opposition party legislators and among the bureaucracy. The former saw privatization as a threat to patronage jobs they could offer when in power; the latter as a threat to perquisites and position. In order to dispose of the enterprises, a mechanism for transfer from the state to private hands had to be created in the absence of any consensus within the government on the management of the program. In February 1985, a national commission was appointed by cabinet resolution to be the final arbiter of sales recommendations. As part of the management structure for the sales, a trust (FINTRA) was established, based upon local currency accumulations of the A.I.D. mission. The commission's job was to offer the enterprise for sale; if there were no bidders from the private sector, the trust would buy the enterprise from CODESA and would become the selling agent. The commission, some of whose members had personal political agendas in accepting membership on it, failed to carry out the task for which it was appointed and, after a year and a half, was virtually cut out of the sale process.

The initial problem turned on the valuation of companies to be sold. It had been agreed that the controller general would be called upon to set the prices. The method he employed (beginning with the original price, to which operating losses, adjusted for devaluation of the colon, less a small depreciation, was added) resulted in a heavily inflated selling price that bore little relation to the current market price of the firms.

To support the privatization program, the mission agreed to use up to $140 million of local currency accumulation to permit the trust to make up the difference between the controller's valuation and the ultimate selling price of the firm. Since the government wanted above all to avoid monetizing this local currency, the plan was to reduce CODESA's debt through a bookkeeping entry at the Central Bank, balancing off the debt of the companies being sold with the local currency made available. The mission had not, however, counted on this excessive level of valuation, and it became clear that the mechanism could not work as envisaged. After a number of acrimonious meetings between the mission, FINTRA, and the members of the commission, attempts were made to strengthen FINTRA and make it more independent of A.I.D.

The decision was finally made to call upon an expert consultant, paid for by the mission, to attempt to solve the impasse. Approaching the problem from the point of view of the political relationships involved, he saw it as his task to establish a low profile, supportive relationship with the key people in the government in order to influence the decision-making process on privatization by working closely with them. His eventual success in doing this was in large part responsible for later progress in getting the divestment process under way.

He was gradually able to establish the government's confidence in him as it became clear that his perspective was 75 percent that of the government and 25 percent that of the mission. Through a lengthy process of negotiation, he was ultimately able to persuade the commission and CODESA to proceed toward the same goals. The government's goals were clear: (1) to avoid monetization of the large sum of local currency, (2) to cut the debt of CODESA, and (3) to privatize. Of these, the first was clearly of greatest importance since the accumulation of the generated counterpart funds in the Central Bank had become a source of embarrassment to the government.

Internal Politics and Privatization

Arias's position on privatization was clear. He was prepared to sell shares in the firms CODESA held not only to bring about reform of their operations but also to democratize ownership through sale of stock to the public. Privatization, if successful, would achieve a presidential objective of broadening Arias's political base, at the expense of the opposition, by creating a constituency of those who benefited from share purchase.

Costa Rica is a democratic country, with an operating opposition party structure, a relatively highly educated population, and a high quality of life. President Arias had become convinced by a visit to Margaret Thatcher in May 1987 of the advantages of privatization—both political and economic. Creation of a larger political constituency by democratizing ownership through stock holdings fit closely with the president's desire to work toward a centrist position to counter his right wing opposition.

However, the Costa Rican situation has a peculiarity that will affect the democratization process. The system has for a considerable period in the past relied on the Solidarity movement as a vehicle for social change. The movement, which embraces coops covering the entire country, would provide a method of distributing shares in divested firms that would ultimately reach large numbers of coop members as potential buyers. Accordingly, the president sent a letter to between 400,000 and 500,000 coop members urging them to buy shares directly through their coops for the sale of the sugar producing firm, CATSA.

The coop movement is fractured between moderate and liberal political positions; the far left has considerable political and economic power within the governing structure since a very substantial portion of Costa Rica's three million people are members of coops, particularly in the rural areas. The president's political goal in privatizing was to set a median course between two evils: accretion of power to the extreme left through control of divested industries by purchase of shares by left wing controlled coops and accretion of wealth in the hands of a few by allowing wealthy individuals to acquire substantial holdings in divested state-owned firms.

The left, however, recommended that CATSA be run as a type of super-coop, rather than as a fully privatized firm. However, the coops have, in Costa Rica as elsewhere, the reputation of being poorly managed, underfinanced, not profit-oriented, and disorganized. The governing party has maintained that CATSA should be run as an example of how a private company should operate; the only way this can be accomplished is by making coops shareholders in a private company that has a largely autonomous management.

The political objective of privatization, then, became clear. Presidential social objectives of bringing about change and reform in the economic system would be accomplished by democratization of ownership—but not democratization in the larger sense of the term implying individual ownership of shares. Rather, what was implied was ownership through membership in the coops of the Solidarity movement. The coops would provide a more solid political base for the president than would individuals, and they would be easier to persuade or even control. There was the risk that privatization could serve to increase the power of the left-dominated coops, but the president took the position that this risk would be substantially reduced if the opposition idea of one large company run as a super-coop could be defeated.

Opposition to privatization came also from another quarter. Within a few months after the the government announced plans to privatize parts of the public services sector, open trade union opposition arose. Union heads argued that privatization was not in the interests of labor, basing their arguments largely on the assumption that transfer of services to the private sector would cause loss of jobs and of employment guarantees now enjoyed by workers. Privatizations that involved worker participation in the management of the new firms generated some enthusiasm on the part of small groups of employees. But the unions claimed that the new privatized services were being established without adequate union consultation. Six central unions formed a permanent workers' council, which requested the legislative assembly to cease privatization efforts in areas considered strategic for social and economic development, such as banking, energy, health, communications, and transportation.

President Arias, with the help of his minister of planning, fulfilled the role of the leader committed to privatization. His influence was able to diminish union opposition to privatization from late 1987 on, but the privatizing process continued to be slow in view of the political pitfalls built into it.

The Role of the Donor in Privatization

The role of A.I.D. in Costa Rica was a complicated one. In its eagerness to pursue a privatization program, the mission ran the risk of getting out in front of both the government and public opinion. Not only was time needed to reduce political barriers, but an educational process also was required to overcome the skepticism of the potential share owners, the coop leadership. It became increasingly important to demonstrate that privatization was a Costa Rican government program, which had the full support of the majority party and that it was not a goal being pushed upon the government by an external agency. Moreover, it had to be transparent that the consultant furnished by A.I.D. had to be obviously first and foremost at the service of the government, acting only as a liaison with the mission.

To dilute the prominence of its role in the privatization process, A.I.D. was interested in having the British play a part. A representative of the Adam Smith Institute in London was invited to prepare a report on future privatizations in Costa Rica. The report recommended a number of possible companies to privatize, including the telephone company. These privatizations would be done with the assistance of British investment bankers and with support from the A.I.D. mission. It is unlikely, however, that the government will be interested in further privatization until it disposes of all the companies held by CODESA, particularly in view of the adverse political reaction to attempts to privatize parts of the national electric company in 1988.

By late 1988, only three major companies remained to be divested, CATSA, a sugar mill that was to be sold to the private cooperative sector; FERTICA, a fertilizer plant, 40 percent of whose shares were to be sold; and CEMPASA, a cement plant, in which an equal percentage of shares were to be divested. In the case of CATSA, the company was restructured into a profitable business by FINTRA and, after some early problems, is likely to be sold to several large cooperatives. Any remaining shares will be put through the securities exchange.

FERTICA shares were originally to be sold to a Norwegian company, Norsk Hydro, and a letter of intent was signed to permit the sale and negotiation of a management contract. However, the possibility of political backlash because of sale to a multinational caused the government to renege on the agreement. The government then planned to transfer the shares of FERTICA to FINTRA, which would arrange the sale of 40 percent of the shares to a wide group of Costa Rican investors that will likely include employees and some users of the firm's products. Political sensitivities were particularly strong in this case since Costa Rican agriculture is strongly impacted by FERTICA's pricing policies, and there is fear of unemployment resulting from privatization of the company.

CEMPASA, a well-managed and profitable firm, has been left to the last because FINTRA's attention has been devoted to the other two, but it is expected that CEMPASA will be restructured and offered in the same way as the preceding firms.

The government will continue to have political difficulties with privatization not only from the left but also from the old guard of Arias's own party, which was committed to the idea of CODESA as a holding company from the very beginning. The government is particularly anxious, however, to complete the sale of 40 percent of FERTICA before the end of its term of office in 1990, but if a reasonable price is to be obtained, FINTRA will probably require more time to reorganize the firm into a profitable operation.

Lessons from the Costa Rican Experience

The Costa Rican privatization program was clearly stimulated by the early interest of the A.I.D. mission, but substantial politically motivated delays were encountered at the early stages. It clearly was designed to have an important social and economic effect on the country, but at the same time it was meant to support the desire of the president to enlarge and solidify his party's political base through democratization of ownership in the peculiar circumstances of the Costa Rican internal political structure.

The privatization process would have been made easier if greater thought had been given initially to the political implications involved in a privatization program. The program was put in place too hurriedly without, it would appear, sufficient consultation with the interested parties or at least consideration of the intricacies of the local political situation. Technical errors were made in establishing FINTRA, and the whole process was made needlessly complicated by the establishment of the commission as an added layer of bureaucracy. Nevertheless, the accusation that too high a price was paid in local currency for firms to be divested is unfair. The chief point to be kept in mind is that the government's primary concern was to avoid monetizing any of the local currency balance so that what might have appeared to be an excessively high valuation in local currency is beside the point. The price was a bookkeeping transaction that served to lower the available local currency balance and concomitantly reduced pressure on the government to monetize any of it.

TUNISIA: INSTITUTIONAL DEVELOPMENT FOR PRIVATIZATION

Introduction

Tunisia has had a long-standing interest in privatization, beginning during the Bourghiba regime and continuing into the Ben Ali government. Most of the SOEs required subsidies that were proving to be an ever greater burden on an already strained national budget. Even more important was the need to increase the efficiency of firms engaged in export production in the light of the government's hope of greater entry into the European Common Market. Privatization, leading to a greater place for the private sector and reduction of the role of the state in the economy, was a major step forward in the government's planning.

The Decision to Privatize

The government made the formal decision to embark on a privatization program in 1986. Legislation was passed in 1987 (Law 87-47 of August 2; full text is in the *Journal Officiel* of August 14, 1987) formally setting up the commissions under which the restructuring of public sector enterprises (including privatization) would be accomplished.

Within the Sixth Plan of economic and social development, the law provided for creation by decree of a list of firms to be restructured. A seven member restructuring commission, composed of bureaucrats, was named to carry out the provisions of the law. Its major task was to evaluate the industries to be divested, completely or partially, according to currently used methods. The commission was free to consult with any experts it desired.

The commission's work was to be reported to a second interministerial commission that was to authorize, based on this report, the actions necessary to carry out the privatization. In turn, these actions were to be implemented by the Ministry of Finance and the ministry responsible for the industry being divested.

To add to this already cumbersome structure, a third commission was created whose job was to implement the decisions of the interministerial commission as they applied to future stock offerings. It was attached to the stock exchange. This commission was charged with seeing that the shares of the firm were listed on the exchange and with providing prospective share buyers with all the necessary information on the financial and technical aspects of the firms. The privatization law detailed the special conditions applying to small investors, who were to be given priority buying rights. In those cases where shares were to be distributed free to employees as part of the privatization agreement, the shares were required to be held for two years before they could be sold. The law also specified the taxes from which privatized firms would be exempt for a period of five years after the sale by stock offering and special financial arrangements that could be used to pay for the shares purchased.

The 1987 law was the result of almost two years of reflection and debate, both public and within the ruling party. Since Tunisia operated under a one party system, there was no question of strong party differences based on philosophy or ideology as in the case of Jamaica. Nevertheless, there was substantial disagreement within party factions between those who believed wholeheartedly in encouragement of the private sector through privatization and those who felt that a strong case could still be made for state intervention in the productive sector of the economy. Both sides overstated their case in the debate; those who argued for immediate and total privatization of all state-owned enterprises were clearly out of touch with the political realities of the country. Those who argued, on the other hand, against any privatization for ideological or personal reasons were equally out of touch with the trend in government thinking on the necessity of dismantling the structure of subsidies.

The passage of the law on restructuring public enterprises was an indication of the government's determination to reduce the size of the public sector. It rapidly became evident, however, that the three-tiered commission structure was more of a hindrance to privatizing than a help. The implementation process was too complex and time consuming, and the consent of too many bodies was required before implementation. Coordination of the work of three commissions required a degree of staff support that was not available. Members of the commissions had no special knowledge of the privatizing process and were often at a loss to know what action to take. They were, in any case, often busy with their own full-time jobs, leaving little time for consideration of the complex problems of valuation of firms or seeking out prospective buyers. No priorities for divestment were laid down and no overall strategy was developed. As a result, little had been accomplished in the months before the overthrow of the Bourghiba regime.

The Ben Ali government that assumed power in November 1987 was more eager to get on with divestment than was its predecessor. Its first step was to make way for a new and streamlined decision-making procedure. Under Law 89-9 of February 1989, the former commissions were replaced by a single body, the Commission for the Restructuring of Public Enterprises (CAREPP), consisting of five members, the ministers of finance, planning, public service, and social affairs, and the head of the Central Bank. The commission is chaired by the prime minister or his representative. The minister responsible for the firm under discussion (Ministre de la Tutelle) at the commission's monthly meeting sits as a temporary member.

The prime minister, on the recommendation of CAREPP, makes decisions on privatizing or restructuring. Forty-five decisions have been made since the commission was formed. CAREPP bases its recommendations on a brief document (tableau de bord) that is produced by a technical commission (CTAREP) headed by the director general of public enterprises. The document consists of a review of the financial and technical position of the firm, capital resources, cash flow, and market position as well as other pertinent details, depending on the individual case. CTAREP makes recommendations for the commission's consideration on the form of divestment. In the process of gathering the necessary information, interviews are held with the firm's management, officials of the responsible ministry, bankers, and any other interested parties. Recommendations to the prime minister are usually made in one meeting, unless more information is desired, in which case the commission can summon the firm's manager or other officials (such as officers of the stock exchange) to meet with it.

Cases are brought before the commission by the various responsible ministries, but priority is given to those brought by the prime minister or the president. An overall criterion applied by the commission is that, if the state is to disengage from an industrial activity, there must exist a competitive situation so that a public monopoly is not simply replaced by a private one. So, for example, the Societe Tunisienne d' Electricite et de Gaz (STEG) is not likely to be privatized because no competition exists, as well as for reasons of national security. While the government would be happy to dispose of the phosphate mines at Gafsa, no private buyer is likely to come forward prior to major restructuring.

The presence of the minister of social affairs on the commission is indicative of one of the government's major concerns. The ministry is expected to provide input on the question of potential unemployment that may result from a privatization action. The government is most anxious to avoid political pressures stemming from an increase in the current high level of unemployment, and every effort is made to see that displaced workers have job opportunities open to them.

In a few cases, such as the sale of supermarkets in which bank loans are guaranteed by the government, the employment issue is not critical, and the banks may proceed to foreclose if necessary. In other cases, such as the Gafsa phosphate mines, the goal is to reduce the present overemployment by attrition. One major privatization, a refrigerator manufacturing company, has been held up by a condition attached to the sale that the buyer employ all of the current work force. Buyers find this condition unacceptable and it is unlikely that the sale will be completed until some way is found around it.

Not all firms to be privatized are money losers; a tourist agency that had been losing money became profitable over the past two years. The decision to privatize in this case was based on the view that it was simply not a business the government should be in.

Unlike other privatization programs, the commission does not operate from a public list of firms to be privatized nor is there a strategy of privatizing large firms or those losing the most money at the outset. Experience with the list of state-owned firms made public under the earlier privatization law was unsatisfactory in that firms not appearing on the list assumed that they were not to be part of the program even when they were losing money heavily. In consequence, they felt that they could continue the inefficient financial and management practices that had made subsidies necessary. The new commission made clear that all state-owned firms were candidates for restructuring; any one of them could become the focus of the commission's attention at any time. Management was thus encouraged to greater efficiency in the expectation that the restructuring secretariat could knock on the door at any time.

CAREPP has clearly streamlined the process of privatization, at least at the top level of the government. Its restricted membership, access to the highest authority, and limited documentation has made decisions on the form of divestment both rapid and simple.

The weakest link in the institutional structure for privatization is at the point of implementation. It is sometimes difficult to avoid the tendency to confuse policy decision with policy implementation. In principle, there is a clear line of follow-up to a decision by the prime minister. It is transmitted to the ministry responsible for the enterprise and that ministry is thereby charged with its implementation. The ministry is expected to make reports on steps taken toward divestment.

If the commission has attached conditions that are particularly difficult to fulfill (such as employment of all current workers), finding an individual buyer may not be possible. The process of working out details of a stock offering (share price, employee purchase preference, and sale timing) can consume substantial time. Implementation may depend on the efficiency and knowledge of the members of the minister's cabinet and the amount of time they may have to spend on the subject. What may be needed most, however, is a senior staff member of the prime minister's office who bears the authority of the commission and whose job it is to devote time to follow-up details and negotiations. Without this support, the streamlining of decisions is unlikely to bring about the expected results.

The Role of the Donor Mission in Tunisian Privatization

The U.S.A.I.D. mission in Tunis supported the government's desire for a privatization program from the outset. It furnished technical assistance, consultation services, and confidential advice on the privatization process and on macroeconomic policy changes to facilitate privatization.

In April 1987 the mission provided financial support to an international conference on privatization organized by the Institute of Management, which drew on experts from Europe, the Middle East, and the United States. The purpose of the conference was essentially consciousness raising on the issue of privatization for civil servants, the private sector, and the public in general. The conference achieved wide press coverage and succeeded in raising the level of knowledge and interest in the topic throughout the country. Papers prepared for the conference were circulated both inside and outside the government.

The government's decision to pursue privatization as a major policy was made more concrete with the passage of the privatization law a few months later, followed by the creation of the implementing commissions. The change in government produced no reversal of the government's determination to privatize. Over the following months, the government's needs in technical assistance became clearer, and the mission prepared a project designed to direct resources to CTAREP, other government agencies, and the stock exchange to assist in planning and organizing privatizations.

The project, embodied in a Memorandum of Understanding (MOU) signed in March 1988 with the prime ministry of the new government, was divided into five components:

- *Preparation*: Financing would be provided for consultant assistance in selecting and preparing companies for privatizing.

- *Asset Valuation*: Technical assistance would be provided from both foreign and Tunisian sources to assist the commission in selecting appropriate valuation methods and in company analysis.

- *Marketing*: Technical assistance would be made available in selecting methods of sale, preparation of sale promotion materials for potential buyers, and on marketing strategy.

- *Financing*: Technical assistance would be offered to promote domestic financial market development as part of the privatization effort. A conference on this subject, using outside experts, was organized in May 1988 as part of the program.

- *Follow-up*: This part of the program was designed to monitor postprivatization actions by the government and the private sector so that errors could be rectified and appropriate actions taken to keep the privatization program responsive.

Detailed implementation of the assistance program also envisaged training in stock market mechanics, financial analysis and corporate finance (both inside and outside the country), visits of stock market officials to foreign stock exchanges, and training seminars.

It was agreed that A.I.D. would recruit and pay two long-term (2 year) consultants but that they would be responsible to Tunisian authorities. One of these, a privatization specialist, would be stationed in the Office of the Prime Minister. This specialist would directly assist the CAREPP with advice on policies and procedures in the privatization program, on organization and operation of the commission itself, and on short-term consultants to be hired for specific tasks requested by the commission. The other consultant, a financial markets specialist, would provide technical and management assistance to promote the organizational development and institutional capacity of the stock exchange. In addition, this specialist would be expected to advise on new financial instruments for the Tunisian financial markets and assist in preparing offering prospectuses for firms being divested as well as individual company reports and investor information.

Finding a senior consultant with the requisite skills and language competence did not prove easy. To be of most help, consultants would have to gain the fullest confidence of the most senior Tunisian officials since the consultant would be dealing in areas of high political sensitivity and would be privy to information few individuals in the country might have.

As part of the program under the project, a second conference on privatization under Tunisian sponsorship, with mission financial assistance, was held in April 1988. The objective was no longer to discuss the philosophy or desirability of privatization (government policy was assumed to be fully determined) but rather practical training in the nuts and bolts of the privatization process, using case histories of completed privatizations in France and Turkey. A Tunisian case was also used as an illustration of the preparation of a firm for privatization.

By early 1989 CAREPP had taken a substantial number of decisive actions, ranging from a number of outright privatizations and decisions to privatize components of some SOEs to restructuring in preparation for privatization. Four hotels, a tile factory, and a flour mill had been sold. Companies identified for either divestiture of components or progressive privatization included the nationalized fishing industry's trawler operations and state-owned shares of two consumer goods factories, which will be placed on the stock market.

Lessons Learned from the Tunisian Experience

The A.I.D. mission was able to contribute substantively to Tunisia's privatization efforts through support for greater public awareness of the benefits of reducing the public sector. Technical assistance has been programmed in direct response to the expressed needs of the government, yet with the understanding that there were many parts of the privatization process that the Tunisians felt they could handle themselves.

The mission's success in assisting Tunisia to develop institutional capability in privatization is attributable to:

• Early support of Tunisian interest in the subject and a willingness to assist the government in its public education campaign.

• Support for and interest in the project from the top of the mission and development of a relationship of confidence between high authorities of the government and mission officers. The government was able to deal with the same officers over a long period so that there was a clear understanding of the technical assistance needed.

- The mission did not get ahead of the government at any time in planning for privatization. While the process did not go as rapidly as the mission might have wished, the mission understood the political difficulties faced by the government and was content to proceed at the government's pace. Throughout the process, an effort was made to ensure that privatization was seen publicly as a Tunisian program, not one that was being urged on the government by a foreign agency.

- Mission officers listened to the government's expressed priorities rather than seeking to suggest a privatization plan from the outside. Advice was offered when sought, not proferred. High officials of the Tunisian government were engaged from the outset in the selection of long-term consultants. As a result, the government was confident that the mission's technical assistance was disinterested.

The Tunisian experience illustrates the importance of keeping the institutions for privatizing as simple as possible to expedite decision making, while at the same time ensuring that the entire process is closely integrated with the operation of the financial market. It also points up the need to tailor donor technical assistance to the specific needs and goals of the government. It may help to speed what is at best a slow process but even more important, it can aid in ensuring that the government is satisfied with the results of the privatization procedures adopted.

MALAWI: PRIVATIZING ASSETS OF THE AGRICULTURAL DEVELOPMENT AND MARKETING CORPORATION (ADMARC)

Introduction

The decision by the government of Malawi to embark on privatization had its origin in the program of structural adjustment worked out in the early 1980s with the World Bank and the International Monetary Fund. The program was directed toward a rationalization and restructuring of major state-owned industrial operations within the broad framework of restructuring the economy of the country as a whole.

A major part of the rationalization was to be applied to the Agricultural Development and Marketing Corporation (ADMARC), whose basic purpose was to develop and market the country's crop of food grains. Established in 1971, the corporation had expanded beyond its basic function to include ownership of tea and sugar estates and a number of industrial firms. Many of these ventures were not successful financially and the Treasury was called upon annually for substantial amounts to subsidize their operation.

ADMARC's limited number of managers were devoting much of their attention to detailed supervision of ancillary enterprises with which they were unfamiliar, rather than to the improvement of the marketing of agricultural commodities. The corporation lacked the liquidity necessary to purchase the annual maize crop, further increasing its dependence on government funding.

A Ministry of Finance White Paper of April 1986 recommended that AD-MARC's portfolio should be reviewed for divestment to create greater liquidity for its core activities and that the Corporation's management be completely restructured. The government's decision to embark on privatization was a result of policy dialogue originally initiated by the World Bank.

The government requested assistance from A.I.D. in August 1986 to carry out a divestment and restructuring program. The mission responded with a project consisting of two major elements: a technical assistance grant and economic support funds.

The technical assistance grant funded consulting services for the sale of AD-MARC enterprises. The government's consulting contract provided for the services of an investment coordinator (IC) to direct the program and a technical assistance team to prepare a series of special studies dealing with particular aspects of the privatization process. Among the tasks specified under the contract were a review of the objectives of the privatization policy; identification of legal, administrative and financial constraints; and preparation of action plans for each firm being privatized. The technical assistance team determined that the AD-MARC assets needed to be categorized in the light of the aims of the divestiture program. The IC prepared reports summarizing the condition of each asset and then graded them according to tests developed by the team. After grading, each asset was placed in one of five tiers:

1. Full divestiture through negotiated sale or competitive bid

2. Divestiture through negotiated sale or a public share offering

3. Partial divestiture through negotiated sale

4. Restructuring prior to divestiture

5. Retention by ADMARC

The government's divestment committee retained the authority to make changes in the categorization and did so on more than one occasion.

A.I.D. provided $15 million of economic support funds (ESF), which were to be disbursed to the government as the program progressed. The hard currency was to be given on a ratio of one dollar for each three Malawi kwacha (MK) of the value of assets sold by ADMARC. This "carrot" played an important role in facilitating and speeding the sale of both estates and industrial firms. Later, a special credit facility was created with local currency to enable Malawian buyers to participate in the purchase of estates.

The mission felt that its influence was limited by not being included as a member of the divestment committee of senior civil servants appointed to execute the program. However, the government has remained firm on this point, maintaining that this was a government committee, in which the IC was included as an employee of the government under an in-country contract.

The government made clear that its major interest was to divest money-losing

ADMARC assets as quickly as possible to reduce subsidy costs to the Treasury, as well as to restore liquidity to the corporation. Privatization proved to be a very useful instrument to achieve these goals while at the same time allowing ADMARC to maintain a minority interest in most of the assets.

The combination of expert assistance and grant funds was critical to achieving the government's goals. The program as a whole has brought new investment and increased the size of the corporate sector. But it has not achieved a secondary objective, a substantially greater spread in local private ownership of former government assets. Given the current distribution of wealth in Malawi, however, and the lack of an operating capital market, it is unlikely that large numbers of new small investors can be attracted to the market in the absence of financial instruments that will facilitate their participation, such as employee stock participation plans or unit trusts.

The program had completed sales of three companies, two development estates, and seven agricultural estates through March 1989. Negotiations were at the final stages for seven additional agricultural estates and several large industrial firms. Sale of one of the most important of these, the National Seed Company of Malawi, was completed in March 1989.

Privatizing the National Seed Company of Malawi (NSCM)

NSCM was established in 1978 to ensure a supply of high quality seed (maize, tobacco, oil seed, groundnuts, soybeans, and other legumes) for Malawi's agriculture. The seed was produced largely by local contractors under the control of the Seed Technology Unit of the Ministry of Agriculture. The company had a de facto monopoly of seed supply and 65 to 70 percent of its output was sold to Malawi small holders, with a small amount available for export. ADMARC was the company's major sales outlet until recent years, when sales declined substantially as a result of high prices and ADMARC's and NSCM's lack of management capability.

The company was owned 72.5 percent by ADMARC and 27.5 percent by the Commonwealth Development Corporation (CDC), a British development firm, and was operated by CDC under management contract. NSCM was by 1987 in serious financial difficulty. Outstanding loans from CDC and the government amounting to nearly one million pounds sterling were coming due in 1988, and long term borrowing accounted for 79 percent of the capital employed in NSCM's operation.

The firm's management made optimistic projections for its future, provided that it could diversify its product to meet growing local market needs and increase its export capability. However, it seemed clear that financial constraints would prevent any such expansion from taking place.

NSCM's management argued that not only was capital restructuring necessary but that it was critical to recruit an international seed company with experience in Africa and its own proprietary technology to create an increase in NSCM's market. CDC realized that it did not have the requisite technology or management skills to undertake the job. CDC indicated a willingness to convert an earlier loan to the company into equity since the burden of repayment and servicing of the loan would have seriously crippled the company's prospects of profitability. The IC recommended that ADMARC accept the need for capital restructuring and that the CDC be encouraged to seek suitable domestic and/or foreign partners.

However, the government ministries responsible for food security were initially opposed to control of NSCM by foreign investors, arguing that this could pose a serious issue of national security. Given the pressure on food resources in Malawi, with a shortage of land and a 4 percent annual population increase, the government regarded an adequate supply of seed (particularly of new strains of hybrid maize) as critical, especially in view of a shortage that had occurred as a result of seed export in 1987. Foreign majority ownership of the company was undesirable unless the government retained the power to control export of seed according to estimated domestic need. A compromise was suggested by the IC under which the government would retain a veto as a board member on certain issues, including seed export.

The Privatization Process

The process of identifying a likely buyer for NSCM was somewhat less complicated than was the case for other ADMARC assets since a highly specialized company was needed. The desired buyer would need to have African experience, be an internationally known firm with a strong reputation in seed technology, and be willing to inject substantial capital. CDC was prepared to waive its existing rights of first refusal to buy additional shares coming on the market.

CDC and the consulting firm carried out international inquiries, since it was clear that no local firm could meet the criteria. Two desirable candidates were found: an internationally known pharmaceutical firm, which subsequently indicated that it was not interested, and the London subsidiary of Cargill Inc., an internationally known American grain trading firm, which became the remaining qualified buyer.

Cargill had sold its operations in South Africa and was looking for a seed firm elsewhere in Africa. Seed was a product needed by all African countries and Malawi was, according to Cargill technical managers, the most suitable country both in climate and rainfall for seed development. Cargill was satisfied with the political stability that Malawi had demonstrated over a period of years and was already familiar with the country since it owned 51 percent of a Malawi cotton ginning company (ADMARC owned the remaining 49 percent).

Cargill was not, however, prepared to become simply a passive investor. Wherever it operated, Cargill sought majority ownership and/or management control. Its approach to the seed business was particularly suited to NSCM since it was prepared to inject capital without regard to immediate dividends. Profits were to be ploughed back into expansion of the firm, with a view to enlarging both domestic and export markets. Cargill saw the seed business as a long-term (five to ten year) proposition before sufficient new product could be developed to make the firm profitable. Its market research indicated a strong pent-up demand by Malawian farmers for new and more productive strains of hybrid maize and a ready market for seed surplus to Malawi's needs.

There was initial opposition to the sale from some government officials, based in some degree on a lack of understanding of the details involved. Cargill undertook a public relations campaign to convince the opposition of its determination to achieve majority control. In persuading the committee to approve the final sale, the IC acted as a stable point of reference, in Cargill's view, not as a government advocate. The new owners formally took over operation of the company in October 1988, although the last documents of sale were not signed until March 1989.

Structure of the New Company

The major hurdle in the protracted sale negotiations was the government's demand that it retain a 51 percent controlling interest in NSCM for reasons of national security. Cargill would only go through with the deal if it could secure a controlling interest. The IC sought to resolve the dilemma in a new plan presented to the committee for consideration some months later. In it the IC proposed that:

• The ADMARC/government share be reduced to at least 20 percent, with ADMARC and the government each retaining one seat on the board. Voting in the board would be by individual vote, regardless of shareholding.

• Any decision by the company to export seed would require the affirmative vote of these two board members.

• The Ministry of Agriculture must be an active participant in all company decisions regarding seed production. Cargill would be required to make available its technical knowledge to any Malawian body concerned with seed production. (Cargill found no problem in complying with this provision.)

• Any changes in rules governing board activities or shareholding would require the affirmative vote of both the ADMARC and the government's board members.

• Cargill, as technical partner, could take a minimum of 40 percent of the shares and a maximum of 60 percent, the ADMARC/government a minimum of 20 percent, and CDC at least 10 percent. Cargill would agree to invest substantial capital in the company and would commit itself to Malawi's and to regional interests.

After further negotiation, the final agreement on ownership provided that Cargill assume 55 percent shareholding control, with the added understanding that it would invest a minimum of $1 million of new capital. ADMARC and the government would together retain 22.5 percent and CDC would take the remaining 22.5 percent. To maintain its level of ownership, CDC converted to equity part of its loan to NSCM. The board would consist of five members, three nominated by Cargill, one by ADMARC (whose alternate would be a nominee of the government) and one nominated by CDC. The provisions for agreement of both the ADMARC and the government nominees on certain board issues were retained. The board chairman was to be appointed by Cargill.

The compromise finally arrived at satisfied all the requirements of the interested parties. The government secured a technically competent partner, capable of bringing wide, relevant experience and capital to the company and assuming day-to-day operational management. Board membership provisions took care of the government's security concerns, and CDC continued as a minority investor.

Issues Relating to the Privatization

Although ADMARC received no direct cash benefit from the sale, future dividends would be forthcoming from the shares it continued to own. NSCM was strengthened in that it was relieved of its outstanding debt and, under its new management, would be operated more competently; indeed, it is doubtful if the company could have survived without these changes. Conversely, AD-MARC managers who had been concerned with NSCM could now devote more of their attention to the problems of ADMARC's primary business, and the corporation was relieved of the burden of finding additional working capital for NSCM.

The sale involved no further concentration of industry than was already the case. NSCM was a government controlled monopoly before the sale; now it is essentially a privately controlled monopoly. Although there is no legal prohibition against competition with NSCM, it is unlikely that this will occur because of the special circumstances of the seed industry. The sale did not meet one of the A.I.D. mission's objectives, that of spreading Malawian ownership of industrial production, but in the case of NSCM, the government's interest in ensuring needed supplies of high quality seed made wider ownership a secondary consideration. It is possible that, as the capital market develops, ownership could expand if ADMARC's share holdings in NSCM are offered for public sale.

Role of the Donor Mission in the Privatization

Cargill officers made clear that the deal would not have been completed without the A.I.D. program for assistance to ADMARC divestment. A.I.D. provided the technical assistance funds needed for the investment coordinator and his team. The IC eventually achieved the full confidence of the government's divestment committee and was perceived to be a neutral negotiator whose task it was to bring about an agreement between buyer and seller that would be the best possible for the asset, ADMARC, and Malawi's national interest.

The sale would not have been successful in the absence of the incentive offered by the A.I.D. grant. It served to fix the government's attention on the divestment process and make the government more inclined toward compromise since the government needed the hard currency. The grant was important in another sense. Unlike the strictures and restraints imposed from the outside by the IMF, which are perceived as negative forces, the A.I.D. grant was a positive incentive in that it helped the government to arrive at a decision to divest without feeling the pressure of external dictation.

Privatizing an Agricultural Estate: The Kavuzi-Mzenga Case

Kavuzi and Mzenga are two adjoining tea and macadamia nut estates in northern Malawi. They consist of roughly 2,000 acres planted in tea and 1,000 acres in macadamia nuts, with an additional 3,500 acres available for expansion of planting in one or both crops. Kavuzi, a fully irrigated estate, is just beginning production of top quality tea, while the nut trees are approaching maturity, although recovery rates thus far have been poor. Prior to the recent sale, the estates were fully owned as development properties by ADMARC. Except for sugar estates, they were the most valuable of the corporation's agricultural holdings, and substantial investment both in time and money had been made in them. Some observers felt that much of this investment was wasted through AD-MARC's failure to accept expert advice in development and management of the estates.

In its final report on divestment, the technical assistance team recommended the estates be put in tier 1 of the priority categories established under the technical assistance contract—that is, that they be divested immediately in their entirety. The divestment committee agreed, ruling out any restructuring or rehabilitation of the estates prior to sale. While ADMARC had done a good job in its development of the estates thus far, it was felt that the private sector was both willing and able to complete the task. ADMARC acknowledged that it had neither the financial, managerial, nor technical resources to put into further development of the estates.

The Privatization Process

Since ADMARC had already made a substantial investment in the two estates, it was particularly important to have an accurate and fair valuation of the properties. A valuation model was prepared based on projected and discounted cash flow models. From this a range of values was generated, using different assumptions on yield, operating costs, and foreign exchange rates.

The successful buyer agreed in the course of negotiations to pricing of the estates on a target rate of return basis. This served to increase the sales price to a figure substantially higher than the offer of the next highest bidder. The reasons for this were peculiar to the buyer as a development company, although the buyer later realized that a lower price might have been paid.

The availability of the estates was publicized through notice in the Malawi press and through direct solicitation of contacts in the tea and macadamia nut growers groups throughout the country. Several factors served to limit the number of local bidders—the remote northern location of the properties, low world prices of tea, and, most important, the sheer size of the transaction. One potential local buyer, an estate in the south of the country, dropped out at an early stage because of the substantial investment that would be required, and its feeling that the macadamia nut planting had been overvalued.

Although enquiries came from as far away as Japan, only three potential buyers were ultimately considered, the Commonwealth Development Corporation (CDC), Lonrho (Malawi), and an unidentified U.S. firm. Within a few months, all but CDC had withdrawn. Lonrho's decision to withdraw was based on the belief that CDC would be prepared to pay more for the properties, since it was not under pressure to seek immediate capital returns. CDC was also attracted by the location of the estates and the presence of a tea processing factory. No local buyers were among those in final contention, basically because the estates were a large, complex project, requiring heavy capital input and highly experienced management, and because the estates were not projected to be profitable for several years.

CDC finally made an offer of roughly $1 million for the properties in August 1988 after lengthy negotiations with the IC. The sales agreement stipulated that Kavuzi and Mzenga estates would be bought by a neighboring estate, Kawalazi, that was owned jointly by CDC; a Malawi parastatal holding company, Spearhead Holdings; and by FMO, the Dutch international development bank. The new Kawalazi estate would be owned 72.5 percent by CDC, 25 percent by FMO and 2.5 percent by Spearhead, and the three properties would be placed under a single management structure. CDC's higher price was in part conditioned by its stake in the neighboring estate, which permitted a cost-saving synergistic relationship in irrigation, crop processing, and management.

From the sale, ADMARC received a cash input of $350,000 and retained an option to buy 10 percent of the new company within one year of the sale. Payment was derived from rollover of loans from a local parastatal, FMO, the European Investment Bank, and CDC. Existing CDC foreign currency denominated loans to the government were renegotiated to be made payable in local currency, and these loans were converted into cash as part payment for the properties. These were supplemented by a debt/equity conversion by CDC.

Issues Raised by the Sale to CDC

Local versus Foreign Ownership. The government's priority of restoring liquidity to ADMARC and the prospect of better management and higher productivity from the properties outweighed the question of expanded local ownership. Sale of the estates to CDC, a foreign development firm, was partially offset by retaining a Malawian presence through Spearhead's minority holding. In addition, CDC is committed to indigenization of the management of the estates as rapidly as possible.

From the government's point of view, sale to CDC was advantageous because of the cash price paid and CDC's stated intention to dispose of the property to local buyers at some future date. CDC's strategy is to divest holdings when they become commercially viable and to invest the proceeds in new development projects. Such divestment has, in the case of Kawalazi, an extended time frame, in that the CDC managers estimate that the estate will require twenty-five to thirty years before it provides a commercially attractive return on investment.

A foreign sale also avoided the sensitive question of any involvement of the Asian community in the ownership of ADMARC assets. Sale to local Asian interests was, in any case, impossible, since Asians are legally forbidden to own land outside the three main urban areas.

Since there are over seventy tea estates and twenty-five tea factories in Malawi, no significantly greater concentration of market power will derive from the Kavuzi-Mzenga sale. In the case of macadamia nuts, a single local grower out of a group of twenty produces half the crop and processes it entirely. When Kawalazi begins production, market concentration will be reduced and processing will be spread.

Strengthening the Assets by Divestment. The new owners took control of the properties in January 1989, and within a year it is expected that almost $2 million will have been invested in improvements. Over the life of the project, an investment of $5 million is envisaged, with only 14 percent coming from retained earnings. Infrastructural improvements will include a new dam for gravity-feed irrigation and new macadamia cracking and processing facilities. Apart from physical improvements, the properties will benefit from a reduction in foreign exchange exposure through CDC debt for equity conversion and a potential further reduction if FMO carries out its intention to convert its loan into equity.

In the case of ADMARC, apart from the cash benefit to its liquidity, the sale produced a number of indirect advantages. Substantial amounts in annual operating costs of the estates will be eliminated as well as the need for future capital improvement expenditure. As a result of the sale, ADMARC managers will no longer be required to spend time on micro-management of the estates and on dealing with the cash drains they caused.

One aspect of the sale added to ADMARC's profit as well as producing a hard currency gain for the government. The IC convinced the government to waive the 3 percent stamp tax normally due on any transfer price; as a result, the buyer paid the full sales proceeds to the corporation. Because A.I.D.'s balance of payment support is calculated on the gross sale price, the government received $243,000 more than it would otherwise have gained and lost only a fraction of this in stamp tax revenue.

Although the decision of the divestment committee was to sell 100 percent of the estates, ADMARC management had negotiated with CDC an option to buy 10 percent of Kawalazi within one year. The wisdom of this decision is debatable. The corporation believed that Kavuzi-Mzenga is within a year or two of producing substantial cash flow and that this purchase option would provide an opportunity for ADMARC to recapture some of its earlier investment in the development of the estates.

However, positive cash flow does not necessarily translate into dividends. The new owners intend to use any cash flow from Kavuzi-Mzenga to finance increased overall operating costs from the consolidated estates. Continuing ADMARC involvement is no longer needed or desirable. After ADMARC has seen Kawalazi's long-term financial projections, it is possible that the corporation's board will have second thoughts on exercising its option.

It is unlikely that there will be any significant effects on employment as a result of the sale. All three of the estates have experienced shortages of employees in the past because of their remote location and lack of worker housing on the properties. The new owners plan to construct new housing to increase the incentive for workers to settle in the area. Kawalazi's management has determined that some 400 additional workers will be needed over the next two years, restoring employment levels to an earlier high of 1,646 workers. It would appear, therefore, that the consolidation of the estates will have a beneficial effect on local employment and on workers' living standards over a period of time.

Lessons from the Malawi Experience

The ADMARC privatization project in Malawi produced substantial concrete results in a little over eighteen months. The process has been more rapid and less complicated than in most other developing countries where privatization programs have been in existence for a much longer period. Within its own particular political and economic framework, the Malawi experience affords a number of lessons in privatization applicable in donor assisted countries. Among these are:

- The Malawi experience again showed conclusively that consistent commitment at the highest political levels is required for a successful privatization program.

- The Malawi case showed the value of an integrated technical team to make preliminary studies of individual assets in order to recommend the form and the priority of sales efforts.

- Categorization of assets proved particularly useful in that it provided a logical framework within which to proceed and within which results could be demonstrated.

- The combination of a full time investment coordinator who had the confidence of the government and a technical team that included finance and banking specialists greatly facilitated the divestiture process. The fact that the IC was employed on an in-country contract gave the government the assurance that he was advising in the best interests of the country.

- The donor can materially assist the privatization process through continuing policy dialogue. The Malawi case illustrates, however, that the donor must be clear on its own objectives in supporting privatization, as well as those of the government. If, for example, broadening of ownership and investment opportunity is an important donor concern, this must be made clear at the outset. Spread of ownership took a very secondary place in the Malawian government's view to the desire to get on with the task of divestment. Here short-term privatization goals conflicted with long-term economic growth prospects that depend on a broadly based economy.

- Donor provision of a financial incentive to privatizing efforts, as was the case in Malawi, may be open to debate. The government would probably have eventually proceeded with divestiture in the absence of the hard currency incentive through simple financial necessity. But it is clear that the "carrot" served to focus the attention of high government officials on the privatization process; it facilitated and speeded the decision to complete a sale. Since the government benefited not only from the proceeds of the sale but from the resulting hard currency addition, some political and bureaucratic hurdles were more easily surmounted than would otherwise have been the case, and the acceptable selling price was probably lower. The "carrot" also served to reinforce policy dialogue because the government had a tangible reason to listen.

- The donor can be most effective in a project of this nature by keeping a low profile. The government regarded the divestitures as a sensitive matter of national concern and was, therefore, averse to sharing with donor representatives some of the internal political problems that had to be resolved by discussion within the committee and government ministries.

- The privatization of ADMARC assets served to reinforce the growing interest of the government and of business about the place of the private sector in the Malawian economy. In the absence of a capital market, it became evident to the government that new financial instruments had to be introduced that would permit broader investment in the shares of divested assets. To encourage this, outside donor help was sought to finance the cost of a feasibility study for establishing a unit trust (mutual fund) to develop the equity market and afford the small investor a new avenue of participation.

Selected Bibliography

The literature on privatization is already immense and still growing rapidly. The titles that follow have been selected for general background and for their specialized treatment of topics discussed in the book.

BOOKS

Aharoni, Y. *The Evolution and Management of State Owned Enterprises*. Cambridge, Mass.: Ballinger Publishing Company, 1986.

Ascher, Kate. *The Politics of Privatization, Contracting out Public Services*. London: MacMillan Education, 1987.

Asian Development Bank, eds. *Privatization,—Policy, Methods and Procedures*. Manila: Asian Development Bank, 1985.

Cook, Paul, and Colin Kirkpatrick. *Privatization in Less Developed Countries*. New York: St. Martin's Press, 1988.

Hanke, S. H., ed. *Privatization and Development*. San Francisco: ICS Press, 1987.

———. *Prospects for Privatization*. New York: Academy of Political Science, 1987.

Jones, L. P. *Public Enterprise in Less Developed Countries*. New York: Cambridge University Press, 1982.

Kay, J. A., C. P. Mayer, and D. J. Thompson. *Privatization and Regulation—The U.K. Experience*. Oxford: Oxford University Press, 1986.

Letwin, Oliver. *Privatizing the World: A Study of International Privatization in Theory and Practice*. London: Cassell, 1988.

Roth, Gabriel. *The Private Provision of Public Services in Developing Countries*. New York: Oxford University Press for the World Bank, 1987.

Savas, E. S. *Privatizing the Public Sector*. Chatham, N.J.: Chatham House Publishers, 1982.

Vernon, Raymond, ed. *The Promise of Privatization, A Challenge for U.S. Policy*. New York: Council on Foreign Relations, 1988.

Vickers, J., and V. Wright, eds. *The Politics of Privatization in Western Europe*. London: F. Cass, 1989.

Vickers, J., and G. Yarrow. *Privatization—An Economic Analysis*. Cambridge, Mass.:
    MIT Press, 1988.
Vuylsteke, Charles, Helen Nankani, and R. Candoy-Sekse. *Techniques of Privatization
    of State-Owned Enterprise*. World Bank Technical Paper, no. 88, 3 vols. Wash-
    ington, D.C.: World Bank, 1988.

ARTICLES AND PAPERS

Aylen, Jonathan. "Privatization in Developing Countries." *Lloyds Bank Review* (January,
    1987): 15–30.
Berg, E., and M. M. Shirley. *Divestiture in Developing Countries*, World Bank Dis-
    cussion Papers no. 11 (Washington, D.C.: World Bank, 1987).
Bienen, Henry S., and Mark Gersovitz. "Economic Stabilization, Conditionality and
    Political Stability." *International Organization* 39, no. 4 (1985): 729–54.
Center for Privatization. "Privatization and Employment Issues" (Washington, D.C.,
    1988).
Commander, Simon, and Tony Killick. "Privatization in Developing Countries: A Survey
    of the Issues." In Paul Cook and Colin Kirkpatrick, eds. *Privatization in Less
    Developed Countries* (New York: St. Martin's Press, 1988).
Cowan, L. G. "Divestment, Privatization and Development." *The Washington Quarterly*
    8 (Fall, 1985): 47–56.
———. "A Global Overview of Privatization." In S. H. Hanke, ed. *Privatization and
    Development* (San Francisco: ICS Press, 1987).
Gillis, Malcolm. "Tacit Taxes and Sub-Rosa Subsidies through State-Owned Enter-
    prises." Paper Prepared for the Sequoia Series Conference (Washington, D.C.,
    May 1989).
Hemming, Richard, and Ali M. Mansoor. *Privatization and Public Enterprises*. Occa-
    sional Paper no. 56 (Washington, D.C.: International Monetary Fund, 1988).
Herbst, J. "Power and Privatization in Africa." Paper presented at the Princeton Working
    Conference, Princeton University, New Jersey, 1988.
Humphrey, Clare E. *Privatization in Bangladesh* (Washington, D.C., Center for Pri-
    vatization, 1988).
Hyden, Goren. "Africa's Debt." *Africa Report* 32, no. 6 (November-December 1987):
    26.
Killick, Tony, and Simon Commander. "State Divestiture as a Policy Instrument in
    Developing Countries." *World Development* 16, no. 12 (1988): 1465–79.
Leeds, Roger S. "Privatization in Jamaica: Two Case Studies." (Cambridge, Mass.:
    Kennedy School of Government, Center for Business and Government, 1987a).
———. *Turkey: Implementation of a Privatization Strategy* (Cambridge, Mass.: Kennedy
    School of Government, Center for Business and Government, 1987b).
———. "Malaysia, Genesis of a Privatization Transaction." *World Development* 17,
    no. 5 (1989): 741–756.
Lorch, Klaus "The Privatization Transaction and Its Longer-term Effects: A Case Study
    of the Textile Industry in Bangladesh." (Cambridge, Mass.: Kennedy School of
    Government, Center for Business and Government, 1988).
Marsden, K., and Therese Belot. *Private Enterprise in Africa; Creating a Better Envi-
    ronment*." World Bank Discussion Paper no. 17 (Washington, D.C., World
    Bank, 1987).

McLindon, Michael P. "Privatization and Development of the Private Sector in the Senegal River Valley." Paper Prepared for U.S.A.I.D., Dakar, Senegal, June 1989.

Nellis, J. R. *Public Enterprises in Sub-Saharan Africa*, World Bank Discussion Paper no. 1 (Washington, D.C., World Bank, 1986).

―――. *Contract Plans and Public Enterprise Performance.* Policy Planning and Research Working Paper no. 118 (Washington, D.C., World Bank, 1988).

Nellis, John and Sunita Kiken. "Public Enterprise Reform: Privatization and the World Bank." *World Development* 17, no. 5 (1989): 659–671.

Posner, Michael. "Privatization: The Frontier between Public and Private." *Policy Studies* 5 (July 1984): 22–32.

Shepherd, Andrew. "Approaches to the Privatization of Fertilizer Marketing in Africa." *Food Policy* 14 (May 1988): 143–54.

Shirley, M. M. *Managing State Owned Enterprises.* World Bank Staff Paper no. 577. (Washington, D.C., World Bank, 1983).

―――. *Bank Lending for State-Owned Enterprise Sector Reform: A Review of Issues and Lessons of Experience* (Washington, D.C., World Bank, CECPS, 1988).

Starr, Philip. "The Limits of Privatization." in S. H. Hanke, ed., *Prospects for Privatization* (New York, Academy of Political Science, 1987).

Susungi, N. N. *The Caveats on Privatization as an Instrument of Structural Adjustment in Africa.* African Development Bank Research Paper (Abidjan, Cote d'Ivoire: African Development Bank, 1988).

West Africa. No. 3691, "Ownership of Public Assets" (May 9, 1988): 823.

Western European Politics, Special Issue on the Politics of Privatization in Europe 11 (October 1988).

Wilson, Ernest. "Privatization in Cote d'Ivoire: Three Case Studies" (Cambridge, Mass.: Kennedy School of Government, Center for Business and Government, December, 1987).

World Bank. *World Development Report, 1983* (Washington, D.C., 1983).

World Development 17, no. 8 (May, 1988).

Zayyad, Hamza R. "Nigeria's Privatization Programme and the Role of Private Investment." Paper delivered at the Foreign Investment Advisory Service Conference. (Washington, D.C., September 1989).

Index

About the Author

L. GRAY COWAN is a former Dean of the Graduate School of Public Affairs at SUNY, Albany, and a former Director and Founder of the Institute of African Studies at Columbia University. He is a consultant to numerous international agencies and is also the author of five books.

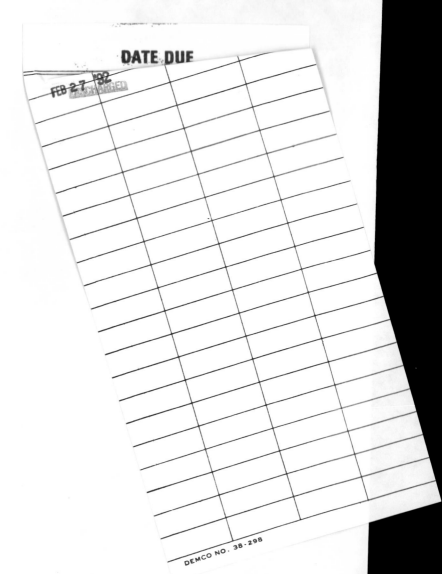

DATE DUE

FEB 2 7 '92 DISCHARGED

DEMCO NO. 38-298